BRI

BRI ᴛᴏɴ
ROCK AND
OTHER WORKS
BY
GRAHAM GREENE

Intelligent Education

Nashville, Tennessee

BRIGHT NOTES: Brighton Rock and Other Works

www.BrightNotes.com

No part of this publication may be used or reproduced in any manner whatsoever without written permission, except in the case of brief quotations in critical articles and reviews. For permissions, contact Influence Publishers http://www.influencepublishers.com.

ISBN: 978-1-645421-72-6 (Paperback)
ISBN: 978-1-645421-73-3 (eBook)

Published in accordance with the U.S. Copyright Office Orphan Works and Mass Digitization report of the register of copyrights, June 2015.

Originally published by Monarch Press.
Gregor Roy, 1966
2020 Edition published by Influence Publishers.

Interior design by Lapiz Digital Services. Cover Design by Thinkpen Designs.

Printed in the United States of America.

Library of Congress Cataloging-in-Publication Data forthcoming.
Names: Intelligent Education
Title: BRIGHT NOTES: Brighton Rock and Other Works
Subject: STU004000 STUDY AIDS / Book Notes

CONTENTS

INTRODUCTION TO GRAHAM GREENE

One of the most prolific and talented writers of modern times, Graham Greene was born in Berkhampstead, Hertfordshire, England, on October 2, 1904. His father, Charles Henry Greene, was headmaster of Berkhampstead School, and his uncle, Sir W. Graham Greene, K.C.B., held the position of permanent secretary to the Admiralty during the greater part of the First World War. The author was educated at Berkhampstead and Balliol College, Oxford. At Oxford he edited the *Outlook* and published his first book, which was a volume of poems called *Babbling April*. After graduation, he held a staff position with the *London Times* between 1926 and 1930. It was during this period that his first novel, *The Man Within*, appeared. Also in this period he became converted to the Roman Catholic Church and married Vivien Dayrell-Browning. In the course of his career as a writer, he has travelled widely; and as a result of his stays in such places as Mexico, West Africa, and Indo-China, he gathered much of the material for his books. Apart from writing, he has taken an active part in the English publishing world and has sponsored certain controversial causes, among which is censorship, regarding each issue from the viewpoint of morality.

HIS WORKS: GENERAL COMMENTS

Although we will be concerned mainly with Greene's major novels, it should be noted that he has also written many short stories, essays, travel journals, plays, children's stories, and "entertainments." His most important works show that he is preoccupied with characters of abnormal psychology and with the analysis of every shade of religious feeling. We shall deal with Greene's religious works in detail later, but the reader should be aware that Greene as a Catholic writer draws more on French influences than on English. In fact, an article in the Catholic intellectual magazine, *Commonweal*, once described Greene as being the first major English novelist who was a Catholic. It is true, at any rate, that Greene had few English-language predecessors whose roots were in Catholicism. Greene's interest in moral issues is not confined to his main novels, however, since similar implications concerning man's spiritual crises can be found in many of his "entertainments." Readers will find, for example, that Greene is among those writers whose concern is not so much with active external events as with people, their subjective emotions and internal reactions. He is also among those few writers whose works are accepted and debated in intellectual circles, as well as being popular on the general reading market.

MAIN CATEGORIES OF HIS NOVELS

Generally speaking, Greene's novels can be divided into three categories, which can best be defined by chronological periods.

1. First Period (1929-1935): During this early period, Greene wrote *The Man Within* (1929), *It's A Battlefield*

(1934), and *England Made Me* (1935). These are rather hard to classify with any degree of precision. They deal with crime studied from a social and political standpoint, and it was in these works that Greene made his initial experiments in dealing with the psychology of his characters.

2. Second Period (1938-1951): We shall be studying in detail the first three novels of this period, namely *Brighton Rock* (1938), *The Power and the Glory* (1940), and *The Heart of the Matter* (1948). These three novels constitute the main body of what we can call Greene's religious writings, and they have in common the central **themes** that fascinate Greene-sin and salvation. By examining man's relationship to himself, society, and God, Greene explores the nature of evil, and the possibility of man's redemption. In many ways these novels contain the elements of crime stories-particularly the "manhunt" **theme**. But their contents assume spiritual dimensions which place them with the best of modern fiction. In *Brighton Rock*, for example, the main character, Pinkie, is a young gangster on the run from the police, a gang, a woman - and ultimately from God. Pinkie seems incapable of loving or of redemption - but Greene takes that assumption and examines it in all its aspects. The "chase" **theme** is also central to *The Power and the Glory*, where a corrupt "whiskey priest" is tormented by a ruthless lieutenant, by his own guilt-and again by God. In *The Heart of the Matter*, Greene examines the process involved in the total collapse of Scobie, a police officer whose warped sense of Christian pity drives him to self-destruction. While *The End of the Affair* (1951) falls into this period, it does not match the intensity and quality of the first three.

3. Third Period (1955 -): It is too early to attempt a clear-cut classification of the novels of this period, which include the *Burnt Out Case* (1961) and *The Comedians* (1966). It is interesting to observe, however, that the first novel of this period, *The Quiet American* (1955), while not specifically religious in **theme**, deals with the destruction of a human being who is apparently doomed by a kind of moral innocence.

GREENE'S OTHER WORKS

An extremely prolific writer, Greene has written many varied kinds of works, from children's stories, such as *The Little Train*, to plays, such as *The Potting Shed*. The body of his works hardest to classify is that commonly referred to as his "entertainments" - called so mainly because they do not deal directly with spiritual issues. These entertainments include books like *Stamboul Train* and *Our Man* in Havana, but underlying the apparent shallowness of many of them - *The Third Man*, for example - lie many of the same moral issues which Greene tackles deliberately in his major novels. His plays have not been particularly successful, mainly because of the pessimistic strain which runs through them. His travel books are extremely interesting, not only for their intrinsic merits, but also for the fact that they reflect the locale of many of his novels. *The Lawless Roads*, for example, is a book recording his travels in Mexico during the '30s. In it we can see the background which influenced *The Power and the Glory*. His book of essays, *The Lost Childhood*, is worth examining, since it reveals much of Greene's personal reflections on religion in general and the theological conception of evil in particular. This provides the reader with a useful background when he comes to study such powerful novels as *The Heart of the Matter* and *The Power and the Glory*.

OUTLINE OF GREENE'S WORKS ACCORDING TO FORMS EMPLOYED

Since Greene has written so many works of such varied natures, we have outlined them in eight form categories, each one in chronological order, outside the period in which each was written.

1. *Novels:* The Man Within *(1929)*, It's A Battlefield *(1934)*, England Made Me *(1935)*, Brighton Rock *(1938)*, The Power and the Glory (The Labyrinthine Ways) *(1940)*, The Heart of the Matter *(1948)*, The End of the Affair *(1951)*, The Quiet American *(1955)*, The Burnt Out Case *(1961)*, *and* The Comedians *(1966)*.

2. *Short Stories:* The Basement Room *(1935)*, Nineteen Stories *(1947)*, Twenty-one Stories *(1954)*, *and* A Sense of Reality *(1963)*.

3. *Essays and Journals:* The Lost Childhood *(1951) and* In Search of a Character *(1961)*.

4. *Travel:* Journey Without Maps *(1936), and* The Lawless Roads (Another Mexico) *(1939)*.

5. *Plays:* The Living Room *(1953)*, The Potting Shed *(1957)*, The Complaisant Lover *(1959), and* Carving A Statue *(1964)*.

6. *Entertainments:* Stamboul Train (Orient Express) *(1932)*, This Gun for Hire (A Gun for Sale) *(1936)*, The Confidential Agent *(1939)*, The Ministry of Fear *(1943)*, The Third Man *(1950)*, The Fallen Idol *(1950)*, Loser Take All *(1955), and* Our Man in Havana *(1958)*.

7. Children's Stories (with Dorothy Craigie): *The Little Train* (1947), *The Little Fire Engine* (1950), *The Little Horse Bus* (1952), and *The Little Steam Roller* (1953).

8. Poems: *Babbling April* (1925).

MODERN CATHOLIC LITERATURE

....

GENERAL COMMENTS

In many ways it is extremely difficult to define exactly what is meant by a "Catholic writer," and Graham Greene himself has on occasion objected to being classified as such. On its simplest level, the phrase could apply to any writer who happens to belong to the Roman Catholic faith. For our present purpose, however, some clearer definition is necessary, to include writers whose greatest works revolve around characters and situations deeply concerned with the teachings of Catholicism. We must, in fact, make a clearcut distinction between writers who regard the separation of Church and Art as the sine qua non of their personal artistic creed and those for whom the spirit of Catholicism embraces their art and molds their expression. For those in the latter category, of course, an acceptance of the realities of sin and redemption and the translation of these concepts into literary terms must be accomplished according to certain tacit ground rules. Such writers as Mauriac, Peguy, and Bloy, for example, could not hold their eminent stature if they allowed their sense of Catholicism to overwhelm their artistic instincts. On the other hand, they would not merit the status of being great Catholic writers if they depicted sin in such a way that they either condoned or were in any way shocked by it. These Catholic writers do not have the function of sitting in judgment on the sinner, nor is it their task to "make a case" for Roman Catholicism in any narrow, chauvinistic way. They are artists, first and foremost, whose creative efforts seek and appeal to a universal audience. When considered as Catholic writers, it is essential that they do what the great French thinker Jacques Maritain told them to do: show a sense of compassion for the sinner without in any way suggesting collusion with the sin.

In this context, then, Graham Greene can conceivably be considered a specifically Catholic writer, when we come to study the content of such works as, for example, *The Heart of the Matter* and *The Power and the Glory*. In general, he cannot be separated from the mainstream of what we shall call "modern Catholic literature," and to appreciate fully his place in this category, it will be helpful to give a brief appraisal of the works of some leading nineteenth - and twentieth-century Catholic writers. The most comprehensive selection of these has been compiled by the brilliant critic Conor Cruise O'Brien. The eight writers he chooses are well worthy of the student's attention, so that Greene's place among them can be properly appraised in the light of what is finest in the Catholic literary tradition. Mr. O'Brien's choice of Francois Mauriac, Georges Bernanos, Sean O'Faolain, Evelyn Waugh, Charles Peguy, Paul Claudel, Leon Bloy, and Graham Greene is as embracing and instructive a list as one would wish for this purpose. While it is not our task to make a detailed study of these writers and their works, some of them are nonetheless worthy of a cursory examination to help us see why Greene's Catholic works are undoubtedly among the finest of their kind.

GREENE AND CATHOLIC LITERATURE

Mauriac once gave his own definition of his purpose in writing when he said that it was "to make perceptible, tangible, odorous, the Catholic universe of evil." While he succeeded in doing this with remarkable power in his earliest and greatest works, *Genitrix* and *Le Desert de l'amour*, his later works such as *La Pharisienne* and *Le Sagouin* are relatively pallid and dreary. Mauriac's own inner torment and sense of class dominate his works, which at their best are prompted by the power of his instinctive, uncontrolled passion. His view of the "Catholic universe of evil" is worth bearing in mind when we come to study the greatest of Greene's works. Bernanos goes even deeper into this "universe," however, to the extent that he sees the world as a putrid, decaying organism; some critics have equated his works with those of Greene in that they seem obsessed with evil in some kind of sick way. However, to attack a writer of Bernanos's stature on these grounds is to miss his greatest quality as a human being, namely courage. For he spoke out boldly about certain aspects of European Christianity which have been suppressed by an over-accentuation on the social aspects of Catholicism. In Bernanos we find the haunting elements of supernatural mystery and terror that we also find to a certain degree in Greene with his symbols of carrion and vultures.

Again, in relation to Greene, we should remember Peguy's famous, oft-quoted, but more often misunderstood statement: "The sinner is at the heart of Christendom." It should also be noted that Peguy concentrates on the historical phenomenon of "Christendom" rather than Christianity. This is particularly true in his long religious poems such as *Jeanne d'Arc and Eve*, where the reader also has the distinct impression that Peguy not only depicts the unconscious, but actually lives in it. Greene's relationship to Claudel is perhaps best examined in their use of symbols, which we shall be discussing later in greater detail, when we study the English writer's greatest works. We mentioned before, for example, Greene's symbolic use of carrion and vultures. In Claudel's poems and plays, the predominant symbols are gold and water, and from the standpoint of Catholic literature Claudel is often held up as an example of the integrated writer in whom the finest elements of art and Catholicism are inextricably fused.

Probably the least "modern" of the list of Catholic writers given above is Leon Bloy, whom Jacques Maritain once described as "a contemporary of Tertullian strayed into the nineteenth century." Yet the fact of Bloy's being anachronistic is counter-balanced by the absolute, apocalyptic fervor and passionate integrity with which he tackled his themes. In this fervor and integrity he can indeed be equated with Greene at his best, with one major difference: Bloy concentrates on bringing the Middle Ages into modern times, while Greene takes modern man, often in his most abject condition and most desolate environment, and translates his plight in compassionately universal terms. Some Catholic critics have indeed been severely critical of Graham Greene's vision of Catholicism, claiming that his attitude is one of extreme pessimism, bordering on hopelessness and, in strictly Catholic terms, that his personal theological attitude is tainted with Jansenism. Defenders of Greene, however, would immediately point out that in novels like *The Heart of the Matter* and *The Power and the Glory*, he has in fact captured the very essence of Peguy's dictum that "The sinner is at the heart of Christendom." For Greene takes his characters stripped of their defenses, and reveals to us the raw nerves of their weakness with a sense of compassion hardened by reality, yet unimpaired by sentimentality. Later we shall study in detail, for example, the element of pity-in its most universal connotation-that runs through his novel, *The Heart of the Matter*. The rusty handcuffs owned by Scobie, the leading character, are terrifyingly symptomatic of twentieth-century man who, in the corroded and decaying milieu in which he finds himself, becomes emotionally paralyzed when faced with human and spiritual commitments he cannot cope with. In *The Power and the Glory*, Greene gives us a whiskey priest divested of human dignity, tormented with guilt, and fettered by fears, and yet invests him with a strange spiritual dignity that is couched in terms at once incredibly universal and universally credible. In so doing, and when judged in our present context, he cannot help but rank with the greatest of Catholic writers.

GREENE AND THE CONTEMPORARY ENGLISH NOVEL

GENERAL COMMENTS

While Greene is a major contemporary novelist dealing with such universally appealing and complex **themes** as man's relationship to himself, society, and God, he cannot be considered outside the mainstream of English letters. Critics have often noted a "decline" in the standard of the English novel, particularly in the last few decades, claiming that it has lost the vitality, scope, and thematic power associated with a Joyce or a Lawrence. Comparisons are odious, however, especially when literary **genres** are involved, since novelists write within a historical framework of which they are a product and which they either defy or help to mold by their works. Greene, for example, does not have the verbal magic of a Joyce or the devouring passion of a Lawrence. But he does not adhere to their world, does not share their problems, does not have their vision; nor do they have his. C. P. Snow, for example, deals with social and class **themes** unique to contemporary culture; Evelyn Waugh treats similar **themes** with the deft humor of an English class often under attack; the so-called "Angry Young Men" have led the way in this attack. While none of this is comparable to the production of someone of Joyce's stature, it does show that the English novel is by no means moribund. Lawrence Durrell, William Golding, and Angus Wilson, to name but three contemporary novelists, have tackled **themes** and problems of vital importance to man and his role in the complexities of twentieth-century civilization. And, while Graham Greene's position as a man of letters has yet to be fully appraised, of course, it can be said now that he has had a major impact on our whole thinking about the Christian ethic upon which much of Western Civilization is based. His characterization, symbolism, and language have placed him in the forefront of the literary, intellectual, and religious scene of our age.

GREENE AND TWENTIETH-CENTURY NARRATIVE

From the point of view of narrative form, style, and technique, Greene is not a revolutionary writer, but is rather the product of the contemporary school which derives many of its techniques from an earlier heritage while molding its own responses. At the first part of the century, there was an exciting scope to the novel, a width of canvas which resulted from a blending of intellectualism, **realism**, and impressionism. This brand of fiction resulted from a world view which was possibly an emanation from, or a **climax** to, the imperial grandeur of the Victorian Age. It was thoroughly traditional in tone. In the hands of novelists like Kafka and Joyce, however, we saw what might almost be called a brief excursion into realms of experimentation which have since had their effect more on poetry than on prose. The modern novelists of Greene's generation seemed to have fallen back on traditional modes of fictional expression, while inheriting some of the more dynamic aspects of the Kafkaesque-Joycean period. There is a strong similarity, for example, between Greene's novels and some of the earlier works of Joseph Conrad, while it would be safe to say that Joyce's Dubliners has not been without effect on the English novelist. It would be wrong therefore, to put Greene in the category of a "modern" novelist in the same way as one would place Ferlinghetti among "modern" poets. Greene is a traditionalist, inasmuch as he belongs to the rich heritage of the English novel. He is nevertheless an experimentalist, since he uses the best elements of that tradition to probe into the depths of the unique problems which beset man in his modern historical setting. In the novel, at least, the expression of the inexpressible seemed to reach an apex with Kafka and Joyce, and Greene somehow deals with inexpressible or unfathomable topics-such as the possibility of a man's salvation in the midst of sin-in a traditional literary expression which is in itself fathomable. The best tribute one can pay Greene is that his works stand on their own merits as stories-he must be accorded the status of being one of the most captivating storytellers in modern literature. In this sense, Greene is remarkably unique and defies literary-ideological categorization.

GREENE AND NON-ENGLISH INFLUENCES

In another section we will be dealing with Greene's place in what we will call, for convenience' sake, "Catholic literature," which happens to be predominantly French. Older French Catholic writers like Peguy, Bernanos, Bloy, and Mauriac helped to mold a uniquely Catholic literary **genre** in which they tackled the universal spiritual problems running through many of Greene's major works. It is also interesting to note that Greene, like Durrell, often chooses non-English locales for his novels-South America and West Africa, for example. He also derived certain ideas and narrative devices from sources outside England-Joyce and Conrad, for example. In this respect Greene is not only a product of the contemporary literary scene, but also helps shape its literary tastes and ideals. For, just as the English novelist at the turn of the century spoke to an audience which had sprung from Victorianism, Greene is addressing a post-war audience which has seen the collapse of imperialism and the decay of Christian values. He must speak to this audience, therefore, in terms they comprehend, terms undiluted with sentimentality and untainted by chauvinism. Even when he picks a provincial locale, as he does in *Brighton Rock*, he is talking internationally and drawing on intellectual, theological, and literary traditions that transcend a uniquely national appeal. Although this is not the place to develop such a comparison, it is worthwhile examining the works of Evelyn Waugh, for example, beside those of Greene. Waugh is uniquely English in tradition, while Greene belongs to the same English tradition, but internationalized and even universalized. Greene's language and style, forthright, clear, and simple, is uniquely English; his symbolism, ironies, and density are derivative of the rich European literary tradition to which Greene also allowed himself to fall heir. His blending of the personal and universal, the inward-looking and outward-gazing vision, belongs mostly to non-English influences.

GREENE AND THE CONTEMPORARY WORLD

In many ways Greene and the contemporary English novelists are paradoxical. While Greene, for example, deals with the ambiguities, perplexities, and complexities of contemporary man's spiritual struggle, his novels are carefully and clearly structured. They are also very short, which certainly cannot be said of most of those of James Joyce, for example. Greene is also typical of the modern school in that he does not draw on a great extraneous fund of knowledge, psychological, theological, or otherwise to demonstrate the vastness of his themes. He reduces one of the most puzzling and complicated subjects, namely man's relationship to God, to the simple terms of a straightforward narrative. Interwoven throughout, of course, are the symbolism, nuances, and implications which elaborate on the tale, leading us to an awareness of the underlying profundities and ambiguities. There is in Greene, as in his contemporaries, a strong tendency to retreat from the vast panorama of the historical scene into a diminished world which mirrors man's spiritual plight. It is almost as if the titanic conflicts which have arisen have forced the novelist to retire to a place more amenable to examination. One of the best examples of this is found in *The Heart of the Matter*, where an intense human drama, encompassing immense topics, unfolds against the backcloth of the Second World War. Yet Greene makes us only vaguely aware that a war is going on. The colony is for Greene a reflection of the historical and spiritual malaise which helped create the war. But Greene can study a man-Scobie-in his colony and give us insights into the universal dimensions of his tale more readily than he can study "man and the universe." Even England's social critics, like C. P. Snow and Angus Wilson, have had to cut down their canvases to size when tackling the "outer" problems that beset modern civilization. Greene's unique accomplishment among modern writers is his capacity to combine a portrait of the inner self with that of the outer world, to depict spiritual torment and isolation by placing his heroes in direct conflict with the social forces around them. We are always aware of the whiskey priest's anguish, but we are never allowed to forget his surroundings.

GREENE AND THE CLASS PERSPECTIVE

While Greene cannot be classified among novelists like Angus Wilson who deal to a great extent with the English class structure, he does deal with it obliquely and in wide historical dimensions. In point of fact, a great many of the modern school do not deal with a topic which is of great importance in England's sociological history. C. P. Snow, for example, deals with class only as a background to the major power struggles of modern society which concern him. Evelyn Waugh, of course, deals with class very brilliantly, but with an air of almost sentimental nostalgia which enhances his novels' appeal but diminishes their value as social commentaries. Greene, however, uses the class of his **protagonists** very powerfully to demonstrate the historical and spiritual climate in which modern man finds himself and against which he must pit all his reserves. Pinkie in *Brighton Rock*, for example, represents and adheres to a lower criminal class in sociological terms. Yet as we shall see, there is great symbolic significance in this, for in Greene's terms he represents a unique type of spiritual desolation to which he reacts in a diabolic way. Scobie, on the other hand, belongs to a decaying imperialist class whose decline is made more potent by his being presented to us initially as a believer in that class. At the same time, Greene cleverly uses Scobie and his corrupt colony to represent the spiritual rot that has gone hand in hand with the collapse of imperialism. Class is again predominant in the background of *The Power and the Glory*, where social ills prevalent in sections of South America are used to highlight the spiritual and materialist conflicts inherent in the philosophies and personalities of the whiskey priest and the lieutenant. So while Greene does not give a penetrating analysis of class structures and struggles, he brings them to the forefront of our awareness in order to demonstrate more potently his dominant themes.

GREENE AND THE "REBEL" CONCEPT

A great deal has been written about the "Angry Young Man" phase of the modern English novel and theater in which writers like Kingsley Amis, Colin Wilson, and John Osborne attacked many aspects of the sham and hypocrisy in the English class structure. Many of the characters created by these writers have been called rebels, but for the most part they can be classified more precisely as dissatisfied men who shout their views loudly, hoping to be heard. Some of the more severe critics have gone so far as to say that these characters are merely expressing a "sour grapes" protest against an upper class they would really like to join. To find the true rebel in the modern English novel, we must in fact look to a character like Scobie or the whiskey priest. They live in a perpetual state of spiritual and emotional tension caused by an inner rebellion against an ethic to which they adhere, and against themselves and their weakness in being unable to fulfill their religious obligations. Sometimes, of course, the characters are unaware of this continual process of inner revolt and counter-revolt, and awareness of the self-destruction this has wrought comes too late. Greene has in many ways captured the essence of what is meant by the true rebel, whose deification of corruption assumes diabolical proportions, tantamount to Lucifer's revolt against God. The Greene hero is in the paradoxical position of having rebelled even subconsciously against the Christian ethic he ostensibly upholds and of finding himself in revolt against the sin he has wooed. Scobie, for example, transgresses a moral law by committing adultery, and thus has rebelled against God. He seeks God's love by an act of pity for his wife which takes the form of receiving a sacrilegious Communion-another act of rebellion. His final act of revolt against God and himself is suicide. Yet, Greene places him in a unique position of innocence, inasmuch as his rebellion can be seen as an act of love. Greene's rebels have every chance of earthly defeat while having every possibility of supernatural victory. Greene sees the modern rebel-hero as a man defeated before he begins, someone who scorns even the results of his own efforts.

ASPECTS OF REBELLION

To regard Greene's heroes as rebels is not something to be overstressed, however, for they can be regarded conversely as extreme reactionaries clinging to values against which society has rebelled. Still, characters like Scobie and the whiskey priest nevertheless both succumb to a sensuality which in a way puts them in a similar category to Durrell's figures in the *Alexandria Quartet*. Sensuality itself is a godhead in Durrell's *Alexandria*, and his characters feel obliged to fulfill an almost sacred responsibility to its creed. They fail, just as Greene's heroes fail to meet the requirements of Catholicism by plunging-or being plunged-into a private hell of corruption.

A noteworthy similarity is also found in Kafka's major figures and in Greene's, because of the obliteration of identity which Kafka does consciously and symbolically and which Greene does subtly and subconsciously. While Kafka's heroes have no identity from the very beginning in the sense of having names like K. and Joseph K., someone like Scobie is presented to us from the start as very much an individual, a model of integrity whose identity gradually becomes swamped by the corruption around him. In some ways too, Greene's characters can be equated with those of Beckett. With both writers we have the idea of identities slipping out of gear, seeking solace in spiritual darkness, and finding themselves outcasts from society. Both Beckett and Greene are deeply concerned with man's downfall, the essential difference being that for Beckett this is a joke, and for Greene it is a tragedy. In some respects, however, the rebels of writers like Beckett and Genet carry realism to its ultimate limits, while Greene's heroes cannot even begin to cope with the reality around them. With Greene, rebellion takes the form of attempted adherence to the tenets of Christendom in the face of a world which has spurned those tenets. In this sense Greene's characters are doomed before the tragedy begins.

GREENE AND ENGLISH FICTION

Greene has been criticized for his lack of experimentation in fiction, and for dealing with moral issues more suited to the nineteenth century than the twentieth. It is true that he does not indulge in bold technical innovations, but neither do many of his contemporaries, nor is such experimentation the prime object or method of Greene's work. The mocking scepticism of Evelyn Waugh, for example, or the startling revelations of Ivy Compton-Burnett both have their roots in earlier English literary traditions and, yet, succeed well in their purpose. Critics have also attacked Greene for not "deepening" with time, in the same way that Dickens developed, for example, between his writing *Oliver Twist* and the publication of *Bleak House*. Greene's novels, it has been claimed, do not have the scope of Tolstoy's *War and Peace*, or the depth of Hardy's novels. It must be reiterated in Greene's defense that his unique place in English fiction rests on the very fact that he has consciously and deliberately opted for this restricted scope. The complexities of modern existence are such that Greene takes a man like the whiskey priest, places him in a locale symptomatic of historical change, and examines the resultant struggles and tragedy. In so doing he is opening up dimensions comparable to those of Tolstoy or Hardy. Both the priest and the lieutenant in *The Power and the Glory* are in their way major historical figures, because their conflict represents one of the major clashes of modern times. In these two characters we see the mounting power of totalitarianism and the declining strength of spiritual values. Greene could not possibly explore the areas he deals with were he to have chosen a wider world in which to place his stories. The spiritual struggles he deals with and the chaos of the society in which they occur are best examined by the method Greene employs. The spiritual issues that face his heroes are no different from those that have always existed. The historical climate in which they occur has changed radically, however, and Greene captures wider dimensions by limiting his scope.

GREENE, ALLEGORY, AND THE MODERN NOVEL

It is interesting to compare Greene's major works with those of Philip Toynbee, who also deals with the **theme** of sin and salvation. Toynbee would apparently satisfy some of the demands made by Greene's critics, since his main works, *Prothalamium* and *The Garden to the Sea*, are much more experimental than anything tackled by Greene. However, while one must admire Toynbee for attempting new narrative techniques in dealing with an old **theme**, it must also be admitted that his works fail as novels. The reader is conscious of allegory to the exclusion of life itself; and, for example, the "schizophrenic" approach to Adam's character in *The Garden to the Sea* ends up in a tedious dialogue. It must also be observed that in being experimental, Toynbee is actually being much more traditional than Greene, since the use of allegorical figures is an age-old device, extremely difficult to bring off successfully. On the other hand, while Greene is traditional in his narrative techniques, his major characters have deep allegorical significance without ever losing their sense of life. The reader realizes the full significance of this unique use of allegory only after being captivated by the narrative. The experience is almost analogous to Wordsworth's "emotion recollected in tranquility," for Greene's use of symbolism is subtly unobtrusive and woven almost imperceptibly into the fabric of his narrative. It should be pointed out, however, that Greene's novels should certainly not be placed in the category of allegory, but that he employs the best allegorical techniques to heighten his dramatic effect. Even his use of symbolism - the rusty handcuffs and broken rosary in *The Heart of the Matter*, for example - is blended so carefully into the tale that it has a kind of "delayed action" effect. It could be maintained that Greene is in fact experimental, in that he has adapted the best allegorical techniques to the content of a novel at once modern and traditional.

GREENE AND THE ATTACK ON SYMBOLISM

In many ways the modern writer has been forced by historical circumstances into simplicity of treatment in order to evoke some measure of meaning - or meaninglessness - out of the chaos around him. *The Stranger*, by Albert Camus, is an excellent example of how the absurd complexities of man's plight can be translated into the most lucid prose and simple plot. Thus a modern writer is given a challenge in some ways much more difficult to meet than ever before in literary history. To meet this challenge effectively, these authors have been virtually obliged to fall back on conscious and intentional symbolism in order to express their point, and this use of symbolism has in turn provoked a strong reaction. Critics of symbolism in fiction argue that the "reality" essential to the novel as an art form is automatically negated, and that an author's scope is made very narrow by his reliance on symbolism rather than on "facts." In Greene's case, then, these critics would undoubtedly censure his use of carrion or rivers or handcuffs in *The Heart of the Matter* as being obtrusive symbols. The point is of course that Greene does not force these symbols upon his novel, but rather allows them to come out of the narrative naturally and realistically, albeit with conscious intent. It could well be argued that a total reversal to a pragmatic approach to fiction would have a far more damaging and retrogressive effect on literature than the use of symbolism has had. Furthermore, to reduce the complexities of modern society to quasi-scientific formulae based on "facts" would be turning a blind eye to the nature of these complexities and to the element of insoluble mystery which underlies the facts. We shall never know, for example, whether Scobie's suicide, Pinkie's crime, or the whiskey priest's transgressions are pardonable in view of the religious context in which they occur. Greene suggests the possibility of salvation, and has thereby evoked storms of criticism from non-Catholic critics on the grounds of the very theme of sin and salvation and from Catholic critics on the grounds that some of his views border on heresy. Greene's use of symbolism is so brilliant, however, that he leaves much to the reader's speculation. And the very controversy that results is testimony enough to the vitality that Greene has brought to the art of the modern English novel.

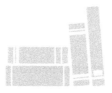

GREENE AND THE HEROIC IDEAL IN LITERATURE

. . . .

GENERAL COMMENTS

One is often tempted to avoid the word "hero" in speaking of the leading characters in modern literature, since figures like K. in *The Castle* or Willy Loman in *Death of a Salesman* seem too bourgeois in background and indecisive in action to warrant the name "heroic." This kind of figure has become more a non-hero, a figure fallen from grace despite heroic and tragic awareness, and this change of stature-seen in the works of Stendhal and Zola, for example-is closely linked to the breakdown of the chivalric tradition and its replacement by a more mundane set of values. More modern writers, like Joyce and Camus, have penetrated the unknown and mysterious areas of their characters' personalities to examine the nature of such non-heroes as Bloom and Meursault. In the history of the English novel, even Dickens, and more certainly Thackeray and Meredith, dealt to some degree with the corrupt, destructive influences within their characters that would qualify them as the forerunners of the contemporary non-hero. Joseph Conrad is ruthless with his characters, pursuing their self-destructive elements with probing, analytical incisiveness. It is obvious, then, that the stereotyped, romantic hero, whose gallant actions took place in a world neatly divided into two camps, one good and the other bad, has now disappeared. Forster, Virginia Woolf, D. H. Lawrence, and writers of that quality have sought more an inner view of man's actions in order to highlight, examine, and perhaps even explain, his exterior behavior. This has been the hallmark of the prevalent tone in modern literature, and we shall see later how a character like Scobie in *The Heart of the Matter* is drawn to demonstrate his inner motivations in juxtaposition to his historical identity. For the downfall of a non-hero like Scobie is the result not only of an inner spiritual and psychological collapse, but also of his being a believing Christian placed in a world marked by the Nietzschean doctrines of man's supremacy to God and by the absence of traditional religious values.

GREENE AND THE MODERN HERO

To use the pejorative term "non-hero" in categorizing the leading figures of modern fiction seems to negate the aspect of the nobility of man's struggle against the superhuman and incomprehensible forces of modern life. The fact that he is defeated does not minimize the intensity of his struggle, and Graham Greene has attempted in his unique way to "resurrect" the hero concept. To do this he has looked back, not to the mediaeval tradition of heroism, but to the Greek idea of tragedy, remembering of course that modern man does not deal with Zeus and Fate, but with broken values and shattered ideals. Greene's major works should be examined in the light of the Aristotelian concept of the fall of the tragic hero, remembering that characters like Scobie and the whiskey priest are Catholics to whom "fall" has the theological **connotation** of a descent from grace. In Greene's works, a sense of **irony** prevails, inasmuch as what man actually achieves, with his personal limitations, is in some ways a scornful commentary on the futility of his attempt to achieve his ultimate spiritual goal. Scobie and the whiskey priest believe in a spiritual force greater than themselves and find themselves balked in their efforts to be at one with that force because of conflicting inner forces and weaknesses. Their reactions to this trapped world of inner and outer tensions would conceivably place them in the category of tragic heroism. Greene has a more difficult task, in certain respects, than his Greek or mediaeval counterparts, however, since the audiences for whom these earlier writers wrote believed implicitly in the religious beliefs which formed the setting of their heroes' actions. The modern audience for the most part of does not have the same unswerving faith in suprahuman spiritual forces; so Greene has to make his heroes' conflicts and settings thoroughly credible. By plunging his religious protagonists, with their human frailties, into irreligious and degrading situations, Greene creates conflicts between the actual and the ideal which makes their fall seem almost satanic in view of the sanctity of their aims. Greene takes the traditional theological concept of pride, exposes it brutally in his characters, and makes the ensuing struggle and **catastrophe** assume classically tragic and heroic dimensions.

THE "INNOCENCE" OF GREENE'S HEROES

One **theme** central of Greene's novels is the unthinking pride which can lead his heroes into a state of self-apotheosis. Hand in hand with this goes his concept that humility before God is essential to achieving true noble stature. This idea takes a unique and at times frightening turn in Greene's hands, for at times he drives his characters into apparently non-heroic and even diabolical situations which strip them unconsciously of pride and drive them toward God. The agnostic Agent D. in The Confidential Agent, for example, is closest to God at his humblest moment of failure; the whiskey priest in his most degraded scenes seems to be with God; Scobie's most contemptible actions are directed toward fulfilling God's will. Also it seems that God's love for the abject failure intensifies the deeper the character plunges toward apparent damnation. What one would glibly call "the natural order of things" is reversed in Greene, to the extent that the most despairing sinner is in fact the one who is closest to the most elated sanctity in the eyes of God. So when we talk of "humility before God" in terms of Greene's works, we are not referring to a pious type of non-questioning acquiescence. We are talking rather of a sacrilegious type of tortured dilemma in which the sinner, stripped of his pride - and in this sense "humble" - is deliberately sought out by God as especially worthy of salvation. The unique fascination about Greene in this respect lies in this strange reversal of the time-honored "good versus evil" conflict. Note that in *The Heart of the Matter*, he places a "believer," Scobie, in the midst of "non-believers," the corrupt inhabitants of a decayed colony. The believer, tormented by a virtually demonic pity, drives himself to self-destruction. The non-believers, wallowing in the mire of their corruption, are obsessed with the lusts of self-gratification that make themselves debauched gods occupying a rotting heaven. Yet the innocence of both believer and non-believers lies in their not comprehending the infinite powers of a God whose grace is closest to them at their moments of darkest misery.

SIN AND SALVATION IN THE GREENE NOVEL

Greene takes the concepts of sin and salvation and exposes them to a ruthless re-evaluation. By placing the failed human being in a position of having given up hope and of virtually grown to be obsessed with failure itself, he shows very subtly that this can be analogous to God's own love of the failed person. For Scobie, then, locked as he is within the confines of a human situation he cannot cope with, suffering becomes the sine qua non of salvation. By portraying the whiskey priest, isolated, tormented, and abject, Greene examines how the weak and the poor, stumbling blindly away from and therefore into God's grace, achieve salvation by plunging toward damnation. There is obviously a close link here with the Greek concept of fate. In both Greek tragedy and the Greene novel, a supernatural force aims its power at a character who himself thinks he is undeserving of it and who does not seem to warrant it by any human standard. Yet, by so doing Greene is not so much providing a definitive solution to an abstract theological question, as he is exposing fundamental questions of great pertinence to twentieth-century man. What is the position in terms of salvation of a "believing" man who, through his consuming human weaknesses and in the face of the overwhelming corruption of society around him, loses his faith and plunges into despair? Greene suggests that in such a case, God may intervene and that the person's salvation is assured through an act of divine compassion that defies all human comprehension in its magnitude. This is indeed a paradoxical situation, since it means that in trying to consort with the devil, one finds God instead, which in turn implies that good and evil are so inextricably bound together that the person who seems the most abject sinner may in fact be the most exalted saint. The whiskey priest would thus be seen as one of the Christian martyrs, although everything in his life points to a sense of damnation heightened by his own awareness of his diabolical descent into a living hell. In terms of Greek tragedy, he has been stripped of the hubris which had given him a specious kind of security and has achieved true noble stature, thereby. In Christian terms, the pride which leads to his fall has been replaced by humility through a kind of suffering that is analogous to Christ's suffering.

GREENE'S CONCEPTION OF GUILT

The heroes, or "non-heroes," in the Greene novel are all guilty of crimes against society. But if they are "innocent" in the sense we have previously discussed, what is the nature of this guilt? Pinkie, in *Brighton Rock*, is a thoroughly satanic figure strutting around an England which assumes the dimensions of the Kingdom of Hell. In his dark world, he is a super-hero, with a diabolical power over others and, as he himself dreams, nothing to think about except himself. Abandoned by the world, he accepts this enforced alienation and pays the world back in kind by rejecting it for one of his own creation. His immaturity is in some ways akin to that of Scobie's, with the difference that Scobie represents the law while Pinkie defies it. The fascinating thing about Scobie and Pinkie, however, is not their differences, but their similarities. Both have isolated themselves from a society by their actions, both occupy a world in which former Christian values of good and evil have collapsed, and, in a very special sense, both are pathological killers. Yet one of Greene's points is that society as it is set up cannot justifiably say that Scobie and Pinkie are guilty, since both characters operate according to a set of values beyond the jurisdiction of society. No earthly power can prevent Scobie from destroying himself, and no manmade law can salvage Pinkie from the diabolism by which he is possessed. God alone can deal with people who inhabit a world so totally divorced from that world represented by the society in which they live. If Scobie is guilty, his guilt lies in his inability to recognize that he cannot apply the laws of Christendom to a society that adheres only to the laws of corruption. If Pinkie is guilty, his guilt lies in his inability to recognize the fact that the laws of corruption by which he abides cannot coexist in a society which pays lip service to the values left over from Christendom. But in either case, does this constitute guilt? Pinkie's England and Scobie's colony both symbolize a decayed civilization. Does the civilization have the right to find Pinkie and Scobie guilty of being unable to relate to it? According to Greene, only God has that right, and we are left with the feeling that in a spiritual context beyond man's comprehension, they will both be found innocent.

GREENE AND THE TRAGIC VISION

There is something tragically ennobling in Greene's vision of a God who extends his grace to and reaches out to salvage those who seem least worthy of mercy. It is interesting to note that the priests who talk to Louise and Rose, in *The Heart of the Matter* and *Brighton Rock*, respectively, have some kind of insight into this. Pinkie's warped version of love, riddled as it is with feelings of revulsion and hate, is at least love expressed in the only way he possibly can. When the priest points this out to Rose, we immediately link this with his other observation that a Catholic like Pinkie is in a much more spiritually vulnerable position than anyone else, since he believes in the existence of the devil and is thereby closely allied to the concept of evil. The priest who speaks to Rose expresses his belief that Scobie did in fact love God, despite all external evidence to the contrary. Greene's heroes strive toward God by attempting to transcend themselves and the collapsed values of the world around them. They act in the best possible way for them in a society corroded by injustice, warped by lack of spiritual values, and decayed by a historical malaise. Their personal feelings of suffering derive from their own inner awareness that they are puny creatures, that their efforts can never achieve their goal, and that these efforts are in fact self-destructive. Their very suffering carries with it its own salvation; their cruel descent to hell paves the road to their salvation. We mentioned earlier the relationship of Greene's tragic vision to the Greek concept of tragedy. It must be again stressed, however, that as a twentieth-century writer, he suffers under the handicap of speaking to an audience whose culture is not permeated with deep-rooted religious values, in contrast with classical Greece and the Catholic Middle Ages. He must, therefore, make Scobie's voluntary commitment to God through the act of conversion credible in the light of the incredible reactions that result from this act of dedication. Scobie and the whiskey priest are **anachronisms** who find themselves in a historical milieu so alien to the culture they represent that their tragedy is virtually a foregone conclusion. And Greene can justify their salvation only by making his heroes' position so humanly hopeless that any hope that exists for them must necessarily be of a divine nature.

GREENE'S THEME AND MODERN VALUES

Greene has been severely criticized for straining the credulity of his readers by concentrating on the "sin-salvation," "tragedy-heroism" **theme** in his novels. It has been claimed that while a twentieth-century audience will accept Hemingway's bullring and Joyce's Dublin, they cannot really be expected to accept Greene's Hell and Heaven. His critics have held that by creating a salvation for his heroes he prevents his characters from being fully tragic or really heroic and negates the genuinely tragic quality of his **theme**. He has been attacked, in short, for spoiling his Greek tragedy by introducing a note of mediaeval romance. It could be argued in his defense, however, that if the critics who equate Greene's tragic vision with that of the Greeks turn round and attack him for not obeying all the rules, they themselves are at fault for assuming Greene's intent. This intent could well be that while the "fully tragic or really heroic" figure depicted by the Greeks was indeed possible in a culture which accepted the fate that trapped him, such a figure is in fact impossible in modern civilization. Greene's concern with the spiritual struggle, decline, and collapse of his heroes is certainly aimed at the salvation which he claims is still possible. But it is aimed also at the civilization which has rejected the concept of spiritual salvation. By so doing, this civilization has created a non-spiritual climate which helps stifle the non-hero, the intensity of whose suffering paradoxically enough increases his hopes of salvation and elevates him to a tragic hero of modern, not classical Greek, dimensions. Greene has also been accused of a certain arrogance in virtually making a special claim to having supernatural knowledge. In his assumption of redemption for people like Scobie, Greene is ostensibly encouraging the collapse of values he apparently deplores. This is a non sequitur, however, since even Greene's most hostile critics would agree that he only assumes the possibility of salvation. Can a twentieth-century author be faulted for placing his characters in sordid situations and squalid environments devoid of spiritual values, rather than in palaces and castles dominated by Fate or the rules of Christendom?

THE ELEMENT OF TENSION

Greene's novels are marked by an element of tension, notably spiritual and/or existential in nature. This tension usually springs from an anomalous human situation in which mundane, secular, or non-spiritual values appear experientially more attractive to a character than the supernatural, spiritual values which pull him in the opposite direction. The ultimate, salvaging relief for this state of tension is, of course, the fall and - in the unique Greene sense - the martyrdom of his heroes, sometimes under the most bitterly ironic circumstances. When the whiskey priest offers conditional absolution to the dying American criminal, he is in a strange way offering it to himself. The priest is by any standard more of a criminal than the American, for he is hounded not only by civil authorities, but also by the guilt of having desecrated his vows to God and by the fathomless fear of impending eternal damnation. Yet, in the midst of the sordidness, the ennobling quality of the priest comes through in his offering salvation to someone who cannot help himself. The priest's state of unbearable tension is relieved only by the possibility that God will offer him conditional absolution. We must recognize also that out of this condition of spiritual tension evolves a unique kind of self-awareness, a reconciliation of the hero's self-deifying identity with his new, humbled identity. For, as the priest, like Scobie, grovels in the ruins of his existence, there is a strange recognition of the pride that corroded his soul and drove him to destruction. In Scobie's dying words we can sense this appalling self-knowledge, his last feeble attempt on earth to make God understand that his love may have been of the wrong kind, but at least that it was love. We find the same idea in the priest's defense of Pinkie in *Brighton Rock*. The important thing to appreciate, however, is that this state of intolerable tension is created necessarily, to strip the character of the delusions that have warped his vision, and thereby bring him to the cruel realization that salvation is impossible without humility.

GREENE AND THE MIRACLE

We have already discussed briefly the criticisms levelled against Greene because of his introduction of the salvation motif, thus precluding the possibility that his characters would achieve the heroic dimensions of Greek tragedy. Yet there is a distinctly Greek flavor in much of Greene's works, particularly in the idea of disclosure resulting from unbearable tension. The essential difference between the Greek tragic hero and Greene's, however, is the absence from the Greek tragedy of the "miracle" that completes the resurrection of the Greene hero. Devoid of the vestments of illusion which have clothed his faults, the Greek hero stands naked before a truth that may indeed destroy him. By introducing the element of salvation, Greene falls back on an aspect of Catholic doctrine that many critics find offensive, not from a religious, but from an aesthetic point of view. These critics claim that Greene's narratives are boldly enough drawn to stand on their own, and that the miracle is an unnecessary intrusion on the author's part, vitiating the plot and enfeebling the tragedy. Here again, however, it can be argued that part of the tragedy in a novel like *The Power and the Glory* lies in the very fact that the hero does believe in the possibility of such a miracle. These critics fail to observe that, unlike Catholicism, Greene in no way guarantees the salvation of his hero. In fact, the ultimate **irony** of his novels may rest in the distinct possibility that their heroes do face ultimate damnation. Everything points to the contrary of course - the priest's interpretation of Pinkie's love, for example, or Scobie's argument with the Priest over Pemberton's suicide. Let us reiterate, furthermore, that Greene's characters do not inhabit a pre-Christian world, dominated by Fate, nor a Thomistic world encased in iron-clad dogma. They occupy a world riddled with disillusion and doubt, and their tragedy is probably heightened, not enfeebled, by the miracle that is hoped for but never is assured.

THE DISCURSIVE ELEMENT IN GREENE

Part of the fascination of a novelist like Kafka lies in his conscious ambiguity-his Castle could be Heaven, Hell, or Nothingness. Meursault, in Camus' *The Stranger*, has been "explained" by critics as representing everything from a Christian failure to an epicurean hero. It is noteworthy that Camus at no point in *The Stranger* intrudes to interpret Meursault's actions or lack of action. The reader is, then, left to his own devices. It is also interesting to note how Greene does the reverse, a fact for which he has been taken to task severely on the grounds that, by having his characters verbalize what they stand for, the mystery that shrouds a K. or a Meursault is absent from a Greene character. In the scene, for example, when the whiskey priest argues with the lieutenant that to give a poor man power lessens his chances of reaching heaven, it would appear that Greene is ruining any chance of the priest's achieving heroic literary stature by having him mouth what is in fact a naive platitude unpalatable to the average non-religious reader. Again, when Helen scorns Scobie for his apparently unsophisticated attitude toward the sacrament of Communion, one might argue that Scobie's verbalizing is unnecessary, trite, and from the novel's point of view, damaging. But such arguments against Greene miss the point, for Greene deliberately has the whiskey priest and Scobie mouth the eternal teachings of the Church, and mouth them as if possessed, in as naive a manner as possible. By doing so, he is intensifying and solidifying one of the main points about his characters, namely their innocence, which we have already discussed. The priest's dilemma is made immeasurably more hopeless by his having to fall back on aspects of the theological dogma which he understands in the depths of his soul but can verbalize so poorly. A great part of Scobie's tragedy rests in the childish, immature version of his faith, a version which is irreconcilable with the complexities of corrupt modern civilization. By consciously introducing this discursive element into his novels, Greene is by no means negating his art as narrator. He is rather mounting the odds against characters like Pinkie, Scobie, and the whiskey priest whose torment lies a great deal in not comprehending the scope and perplexities behind the words of faith they utter.

GREENE'S "ENTERTAINMENTS"

. . . .

INTRODUCTION

The novels Greene describes as "entertainments" differ from his ideological novels in their greater use of melodrama, less intense character development, and willingness to use the happy ending. They are more or less psychological thrillers containing acute perception, swiftness of pace, and raciness of style. Although violence is present in these entertainments, it is less intense than in the novels, serving to heighten the narrative and embellish the tone. The big difference lies in the fact that his entertainments do not serve to jolt the reader's complacency or make him ponder the profundities of existence. The entertainments do not have the powerful, long-drawn-out after-effects that his novels have. Greene does not intend them to. They are worth studying, however, not only as literature, but also for the clever way Greene toys around with some of the ideas he develops completely in his major novels.

NOVELS AND ENTERTAINMENTS

In his introduction to *The Third Man* Greene admits his preference for a happy ending in his entertainments. Even then, however, the conclusion is by no means blissful, since the reader is left with the feeling that there isn't much in life left for the people brought together. Their happiness is more apparent than real, and seems to be shadowed by somber events. Greene has been asked why he writes these at all, and part of his answer is that the melodramatic aspects of his entertainments are in fact part of the modern world of terror, brutality, and barbarism. He claims that there is a kind of nostalgia in the pleasure we get from gangster novels, a nostalgia for a life where emotions exist on a level below the cerebral. At one time, as he notes in The Ministry of Fear, melodrama dealing with violence seemed synthetic, but in this day and age the novelist cannot ignore the intrigue and brutality around him.

MORALITY AND ENTERTAINMENTS

Greene's detective stories are like Chesterton's, in that they are used to reveal not only crime, but also the profound problem underlying it. While people like Raven, in *This Gun for Hire*, and Harry Lime in *The Third Man*, are hounded by civil authorities, they are also hunted by what Mary McCarthy describes as "the Eumenides of conscience, by guilt, by the loss of God, the sense of moral implication in the crime that is the modern world." Also on the topic of Greene's thrillers, Morton Zabel says that "Greene has brought about one of the most promising collaborations between **realism** and spirituality that have recently appeared in fiction, saving his work as much from the squashy hocus-pocus or mechanical contrivance of the common thriller as from the **didactic** sanctimony of conventional religiosity." Note that both Greene and Dostoevsky are highly successful in linking morality and the conventional detective story.

CONRAD, HARDY, AND GREENE

It has been suggested that Conrad's *The Secret Agent*, a classic of its kind, is the inspiration for Greene's *The Confidential Agent*. Conrad's great contribution to this particular literary **genre** lies in his having employed melodramatic techniques in a serious way. In Under Western Eyes, for example, he uses this type of novel to show that "the old despotism and the new Utopianism are complementary forms of moral anarchy." Thomas Hardy does something similar, and uses melodrama to outline a fatalistic philosophy and to blend environment and character. In this respect Greene follows Hardy and Conrad, for behind the scenery and props of his melodramas lies a rather extensive world of philosophic and religious content. We can see how this type of approach presages such works as *Brighton Rock* and *The Heart of the Matter*, where the central characters are an integral part of the setting, in a sense, and where the over-all effect is to intensify the religious and metaphysical content. Greene is very subtle in his use of melodrama, however, and in this respect he is much more akin to Conrad than to Hardy.

GREENE AND THE EXCEPTIONAL INDIVIDUAL

Greene is interested in the exceptional character, especially one involved in moral heroism or moral degradation. In *Orient Express*, for example, the essential heroism of Coral Musker and Dr. Czinner is contrasted with the degeneration of Quin Savory and Mabel Warren. Greene is not particularly at home with treating mediocre characters who operate with caution, and it is noteworthy that there is a hectic atmosphere surrounding his heroes and heroines. He is also intrigued by unique cases of bewildering pathology, such as Harry Lime in *The Third Man*, or Willi Hilfe in *The Ministry of Fear*. The motivations and emotions of three characters in particular are worth a brief note; the harelipped murderer, Raven, in *This Gun for Hire*, the scholar-cum agent, D., in *The Confidential Agent*, and Arthur Rowe, in *The Ministry of Fear*.

RAVEN AND THIS GUN FOR HIRE

Note the close link between Raven and Pinkie, both having had bitterly unhappy childhoods. Raven's character is molded out of hatred, and his experiences have made it impossible for him to love. He has felt betrayed every time he has tried to love or to give himself in any way. This even applies to the lawless world in which he lives. His physical deformity embitters him, since the world apparently cannot see beyond a man's face. Raven's tragedy lies in his feeling that trust automatically brings pain. Ironically enough, the only person for whom he lowers his defenses is Anne, and even here he is betrayed, since she is the girl of the detective pursuing him. Thus, his belief that loving is equated with betrayal is irrevocably confirmed, and his life of rejection and alienation is terminated in the only way possible for him. It is interesting, however, that his final, pathetic plea, "Ah, Christ, that it were possible," has the same tone of desperate longing as Scobie's final words.

AND THE CONFIDENTIAL AGENT

Although D. hates as fervently as Raven, his hatred is largely self-directed; furthermore, he is more intellectual than Raven. D. is in some ways a forerunner of Scobie, since his life is marked by distrust-of himself and of others. No one has confidence in D. either, just as the authorities keep an eye on Scobie. D.'s pity for Rose Cullen is reminiscent of the same emotion in Scobie. The guilt and self-hatred that consume D. are based on the delusion that he is responsible for his wife's death, and this leads to his feeling that he carries destruction with him wherever he goes. He is compulsively obsessed with betrayal and shattered innocence; he is pessimistic, suspicious, and has a fixation on pain and death. Yet he is humble and generous toward the innocent, despite his passion for revenge. His sexual attitude is based on his belief that the act of desire is an act of faith-but then he has lost his faith. This explains why he withholds love, and why he cannot really believe in his happiness with Rose.

ROWE AND THE MINISTRY OF FEAR

Of Arthur Rowe, W. H. Auden writes that in his characterization, "Graham Greene analyzes the vice of pity, that corrupt **parody** of love and compassion which is so insidious and deadly for sensitive natures." Rowe's ethic of pity is described by Auden as essentially egotistical, since "behind pity for another lies self-pity, and behind self-pity lies cruelty." Rowe is highly sensitive to pain and will not permit anything to suffer, even to the extent of killing to relieve misery. Scobie and Rowe have, therefore, much in common, in that they are both victims of their pity for the suffering of others. This attitude leads Rowe to euthanasia, just as it drives Scobie to suicide. The major difference between Scobie and Rowe is that Scobie is completely ignorant of the origins of his pity, whereas Rowe is acutely conscious of the process whereby pity and childhood are linked. Rowe's pity is nevertheless adolescent, and he is steeped in a kind of childlike, innocent hope. As a result, his emotions fail to mature into fully developed adult love.

GREENE'S HEROINES

The heroines in Greene's entertainments are marked by a distinct uniformity which is not found among his heroes. Coral Musker in *Orient Express* and Anne Crowder in *This Gun for Hire* are both chorus girls, for example. They are both scared of the insecurity of show business, yet are also courageous and cheerful. Their relationship with men is based on a genuine and heartfelt desire to rescue them from being total outcasts. Dr. Czinner, for example, achieves a certain degree of self-knowledge, identity, and peace through Coral's devotion to him, while Raven knows a brief moment of comfort in the pain of his existence through Anne's understanding.

Rose Cullen, the rich girl in *The Confidential Agent*, and Else, the poor girl in the same work, share primarily the same sense of homelessness in their backgrounds. Rose's childhood was marked by mistrust through her father's unscrupulousness and infidelities, while Else's was stamped by poverty and fear. Still both girls manage to retain a quality of innocence and belief despite their knowledge of the rapacity of which men are capable. Rose and Else both risk everything for D., who is deeply disturbed when he learns how much they both have learned about human corruption. D. believes that such knowledge should come slowly, and that the final disillusionment with human nature should come with death. Rose and Else therefore bear a close resemblance to Coral and Anne in this unique combination of innocence and experience-something found also in Rose of *Brighton Rock*. All four are in various ways and degrees caught in a world of violence, pitying and being pitied in turn by the men who lead lives of violence. The result of their unselfish devotion to these men often takes the form of cruel treatment, but in spite of this, these women still retain a basic faith in goodness.

VILLAINS AND VIOLENCE

Greene admired villains as depicted by James and Dickens because of the atmosphere of supernatural evil that surrounds them. On the other hand, he deplores the villainy depicted by Fielding, since it is entirely of a sexual nature. For Greene, it is essential that an intense moral struggle take place before supernatural evil can come through as a reality. In this respect, it is important to note that such a moral struggle does in fact exist in his entertainments. To demonstrate this, one need only look at Willi Hilfe in *The Ministry of Fear* and Harry Lime in *The Third Man* as examples of the type of villains Greene describes. Both these characters are eaten up with selfishness, and have an amoral attitude to life springing from their sense of the worthlessness of human existence. By organizing terror and espionage in wartime London, Hilfe translates his world view into action. Harry Lime, who causes mass murder in post-war Vienna by stealing and diluting penicillin and selling it to a children's hospital, is indifferent to the loss of human life. They are really diabolical figures who are intelligent, well-educated, twisted, and totally ruthless. They revel in the pain they inflict on others, and murder not through fear or hate, but for profit and even self-improvement.

We must remember the historical setting in which Greene wrote his early entertainments, for in the 1930s there was a great deal of violence associated with social changes. His thrillers reflect the turbulent mood of the times. In *The Lost Childhood*, Greene himself says, "Life is violent and art has to reflect that violence." In many ways Greene is obsessed with the violence marking twentieth-century history, a violence that came for him to a frightening **climax** during the London blitz. That is why violence is represented in his thrillers as an integral part of the human situation and why the inner moral conflicts suffered by his characters are heightened by the external violence in which they indulge.

TECHNIQUES IN THE ENTERTAINMENT

Greene uses certain brilliantly worked-out techniques in his entertainments which serve to capture the reader's attention by his use of **imagery** and of certain autobiographical material. Read the opening two paragraphs to *This Gun for Hire*, for example, and see how Greene immediately captures the reader and plunges him into Raven's world. The opening of *Brighton Rock* does the same thing, although, of course, the dimensions of Pinkie's world are wider and more subtly drawn than those of Raven's. The end of *This Gun for Hire* is also worth studying as being typical of the way Greene draws everything together by having Raven receive the violence which he himself has delivered from the beginning. Greene also makes particularly brilliant use of striking images to set the tone of his entertainments. In *The Confidential Agent*, for example, the opening sets the mood of violence and murder by references to gulls, fogs, sirens, and ships, all of which have certain **connotations** for D. Note how this device is also used by Greene in his novels, probably the best example being the beginning of *The Heart of the Matter*, where the whole atmosphere of decay and corruption is established by such images as the vultures on the roof. Some autobiographical material comes into play at times, as is shown by Arthur Rowe's imagining himself to be an insect crawling beneath a stone. This reminds us of Greene's reminiscing, in one of his personal essays, how he felt himself to be an insect under a stone when he thought of the revenge he wanted to take on a boy at school. Rowe is also like Greene in the way he was raised on heroic tales, his experience of real life often contradicting what he read in books. In *The Lost Childhood*, Greene talks about the thrills and the disillusionment that he received as a boy reading various tales of adventure, and about the disillusionment that comes often from the reality of life itself. The techniques used by Greene in his entertainments are worth studying for the light they shed on technical aspects of his more serious works.

GREENE'S RELIGIOUS TRILOGY

....

INTRODUCTION

GENERAL COMMENTS

Of all Greene's works, the three which give the most insight into his thinking on religion are *Brighton Rock, The Power and the Glory*, and *The Heart of the Matter*. Although the first deals with a gangster, the second with a priest, and the third with a policeman, all three have in common Greene's major religious **theme**: man's sin and the possibility of his redemption. Greene's earlier books show that he was already toying with this idea, but in these three novels he exposes the raw nerves of this **theme** for our examination.

The central characters in these works are all driven to death: Pinkie as a seventeen-year-old gangster and murderer *(Brighton Rock)*, the whiskey priest as a coward and a derelict *(The Power and the Glory)*, and Scobie as a corrupted law officer *(The Heart of the Matter)*. The fact that they are all Catholics makes their position all the more damnable-literally so-since their awareness of the existence of evil heightens their knowledge of their sins. In one sense, then, they have lost their innocence, and it would apparently follow that the possibility of their being eternally damned in thereby heightened. According to Greene, however, the reverse may be true, namely that the deeper such characters plunge themselves into evil, the closer they are coming to God's love and their own salvation. In Greene's terms, these three characters are extremely innocent people whose knowledge of evil only serves to increase their ignorance of it, to such an extent that they at times commit offenses against God in order to do God's will. Bizarre as it may seem, it is possible that the only thing Pinkie could love was evil itself; or that the priest's road to salvation lay in his transgressing what in men's eyes are God's laws; or that Scobie's adultery and sacrilege were the only means he had of expressing his pity for humans and his love for God.

SIMILARITIES IN THE THREE BOOKS

We have already mentioned certain differences among the main characters of these works. The fact that one work has its setting in England, the second in South America, and the third in Africa is a further difference among them. These differences are more than counter-balanced, however, by the similarities which in a way bind them together into a unique of trilogy.

On one level, for example, they are all extremely realistic novels which stand on their own as well-integrated stories. On a deeper level, they are works of spiritual intensity which are at once thought-provoking and moving. And, as we mentioned earlier, Greene concentrates on the **theme** of sin and salvation in such a way that it would not be at all cynical to describe Pinkie, the priest, and Scobie as "heroes" in a literary sense, and as "martyrs" in a religious sense.

Add to this the feelings of fear, guilt, loss, and betrayal which permeate these novels, and we can see how Greene captured in them all the emotions he himself had experienced. They also contain a sense of Greene's own compassion for the exiled members of the human race, and express quite brilliantly the terror that runs through the lives of the heroes. Greene places great stress on the sufferings and tensions of his characters in order to reconcile such pain with God's love. He also shows that Christian teachings are so riddled with paradoxes and ambiguities that they can easily lead a psychologically disturbed personality to pursue a path directly opposite the traditional "path of virtue." Some of Green's characters simply must reach diabolical depths in their quest-conscious or unconscious-for possible salvation.

These novels are works that deal with the inevitability of pain and suffering in a world that has rejected spiritual values. They also deal with a spiritual tension within man so intolerable that he cannot help breaking under the strain-at which point he must throw himself on God's mercy for his own salvation.

BRIGHTON ROCK

....

PLOT ANALYSIS

The plot revolves around Pinkie Brown, the seventeen-year-old boss of Kite's mob, a gang operating in Brighton, England. Fred Hale (also known as Cauley Kibber), a publicity worker for the newspaper, *The Daily Messenger*, had betrayed Kite to a certain Colleoni, a flashy and successful racketeer who also happens to be a friend of the police. Pinkie, as the new boss, must prove his right to the leadership of the gang by seeking revenge on Hale for the murder of Kite. The fact that Fred Hale dies of a heart attack before he can be killed does not lessen the fact that it is murder. Fred has become acquainted with Ida Arnold, a blonde who hangs around the amusement area, in order to try to escape Pinkie and his gangsters. Ida learns of Fred's death when she is in London, and she rules out any idea of suicide or death by a heart attack, since she recalls his terror and his fierce desire to live. Ida returns to Brighton, finds out what happened, and gets herself involved in the gang war between Pinkie and Colleoni. As a result of betting on Black Boy, Fred's horse, she wins some money which allows her to trap the murderer in her own time.

Pinkie sends an old, frightened member of the gang, Spicer, around Brighton to leave Fred's identification cards in various places so that the exact time of his murder cannot be established precisely. Rose, a waitress at Snow's Restaurant, finds a card, but knows that Spicer is not Fred. Rose has to be silenced or "won over," and to do this Pinkie courts her. She falls in love with him. Ida learns from Rose that the identification card was not left by Fred, and she knows then that Pinkie is responsible for Fred's death. Ida now becomes Fred's self-appointed avenger. To obtain confirmation of this role, she consults her "ouija board," which spells out the word "fresuicilleye," interpreted by her as meaning she must obey the "eye-for-an-eye" concept of justice to avenge Fred's death.

Pinkie is gradually pressured into actions that lead to his own destruction. The pressure comes mainly from Ida, who asks continual questions, gets in touch with Spicer by phone, and hounds Rose. The main action Pinkie takes is to marry Rose, thus corrupting her, and to try to make her enter a fake suicide pack with him. Ida is ruthless and relentless in her actions also, however, and even verbalizes this by comparing herself to a stick of Brighton rock, a type of candy on which the name "Brighton" always appears no matter how deeply one bites into it. Ida rushes with a policeman to the cliff where Pinkie is attempting to force damnation on Rose. She saves Rose from suicide and forces the policeman to drive Pinkie to his death. Rose goes to confession after Pinkie's death, and says she cannot repent her failure to seek damnation with Pinkie. The priest tries to comfort her by telling her of Peguy, who could not tolerate the thought that God would eternally damn any of His creatures. He also tells her that a Catholic is more capable of evil than is anyone else, since he is more in touch with the devil than is anyone else. This does not completely reassure Rose, however, whose teachings about evil point to the reality of eternal damnation. Sure that she is bearing Pinkie's child, she goes home to hear a record Pinkie had made for her. It turns out to be the most terrible moment of all, for on the record Pinkie tells her how much he has hated her and everything she stands for. Rose now has confirmation of Pinkie's total hatred, and she is left devoid of hope. Life for her has become something of total horror, symbolized by the very method of Pinkie's death. For, just as the sea swallows up Pinkie's body, the full realization of the meaning of evil swallows up Rose. The sea has drunk in Pinkie's evil, which now has become part of the natural order of the universe. *Brighton Rock* is one of the most dramatic and powerful novels of modern fiction.

ANALYSIS OF CHARACTERS, THEMATIC MATERIAL, AND THEIR INTERRELATIONSHIP

Pinkie-Motivation and Conflict

Having dealt at length with Greene and the heroic tradition in literature, it would follow that in a unique sense, Pinkie is the hero of *Brighton Rock*. In saying this, however, we should remember that Greene's heroes live in a democratic, not a feudal world, and that their very struggle to achieve noble stature makes them heroic. The impossibility of modern man's ever achieving anything approaching romantic heroism seems to go hand in hand with his fall from grace. Pinkie's world can therefore be seen as a kind of sociological hell into which he was born as a juvenile delinquent of satanic proportions. Pinkie can be regarded as a self-styled superman occupying an anti-God world in post-Nietzschean England, a modern Raskolnikov determined to prove his superiority to everyone around him - and to himself.

His obsession with self and the appeasement of his selfish desires obliterates any hope that he can enter into a genuinely compassionate relationship with anyone outside himself. His dream that he might have no more human contacts, that he might be free to think about nothing but himself, is but a statement of the fact that he is willing to kill to achieve the splendid isolation he craves.

Note, however, that while Pinkie is openly defying what he believes to be the values of the society around him, he is in fact the end product of that society. While the Byronic hero and the Russian romantic hero could thrive in a society at least structured on faith, Pinkie is the child of a faithless world. He must therefore accept what he finds, and seek his heroic stature in his own milieu. In a very real sense, then, Pinkie stands outside "the law of the land" as popularly conceived and is "beyond good and evil" to such a degree that he cannot be dealt with according to normal standards. At this point Greene would state that God and God alone can deal with someone as diabolical as Pinkie and that Pinkie's salvation would be granted by a divine law whose compassion for the exiled of the world is too deep for human beings to comprehend.

Greene's use of Locale

Greene makes interesting, symbolic use of locale in his novels, and makes sure that the reader sees how a place appears from various viewpoints. We can then study the spiritual intensity with which his characters regard the world they inhabit, and from our findings arrive at a measure of critical objectivity well-rounded by our having seen that world from different angles. In this novel, Brighton is not Pinkie's home-it is his world. He would be lost anywhere else, for Brighton is very much a heaven to him-in pretty much the same way Milton's Lucifer created a heaven for himself out of the hell to which he and his cohorts had descended. Note how differently Colleoni and Ida Arnold see Brighton, and how that vision differs from the Nelson Place which represents Pinkie's past life.

For Greene it is extremely important that the reader be aware of the total incompatibility of these worlds, an incompatibility drawn into sharp relief by Pinkie's futile attempts to break away from Nelson Place and all it represents. Pinkie cannot even adhere successfully to the sinister world he inherits from Kite, because in a very real sense it is still alien to him. Any attempt to break away from his dark, private world means invading another one, and this intrusion automatically evokes a hostile response from its inhabitants. This accounts for the war waged against Pinkie by Ida and Colleoni, a war of defense against an enemy who is by nature an enemy to everyone but himself.

This idea of the dichotomy of vision by people occupying the same geographical location is found in many of Greene's works. To Scobie, for example, the colony represents something entirely different from what it means to Yusef, and the whiskey priest and the lieutenant see the slums around them in a totally different light. The essential "strangeness" of the world around us is very strong element, consistently.

Pinkie, Rose, and Ida

It has been said that Greene's characters fall into two categories. Scobie and Pinkie, and other members of the first, do not seem to learn anything, while others, like the whiskey priest, seem to come to some form of understanding. Pinkie is bound by evil, and this makes him almost equally bound to the innocence of Rose. The seventeen-year-old gangster knows he and Rose complement each other, but also knows how they are different from their pursuer, Ida.

When Greene says that Ida is far from either of them as she is from Heaven or Hell, he is in fact making a major statement on the very core of the novel. Ida's total lack of comprehension as to why Rose loves Pinkie is testimony to the totally secular world she inhabits. Ida does not believe in Heaven or Hell, in fact, so she cannot possibly see that to Rose and Pinkie the world is a vast territory occupied by two eternities which oppose each other, yet coexist. It is natural therefore that Ida would set herself up as a kind of self-appointed fighter for justice, aiming at saving Rose and punishing Pinkie. Ida simply cannot have any pity for something she is completely incapable of understanding.

Ida and Faith

Ida is, in a sense, beyond good and evil, and her fun-loving, booming personality carries with it the empty moral values of the "good old days" type of concept. Morally she is unconscious, regarding herself as being at times perhaps rash and imprudent, but never wrong or immoral. She creates her own morality, which is, in fact, a cult of good times and fair play that regards adultery, for example, as a part of human nature. Her code ignores God completely, although it does not condone murder. She dreads death, for life is everything to her, and the only indication of religious feelings in her is her belief in ghosts and ouija boards. Justice to her means law and order, in the traditional legal sense, and there is nothing mysterious in her view of life despite her dabbling in the occult. Her blowsy vitality survives on platitudes, sensuality, and a bourgeois morality devoid of any spiritual values.

Brighton's Two Worlds

Brighton consists of two world-that occupied by Pinkie and Rose and the one inhabited by people like Ida. Ida's world contains the vast majority of Brighton's population, however, including members of Pinkie's gang. The philosophy inherent in this world is epitomized by the types that possess it and which it possesses-Dallow, who proclaims that he doesn't believe in what he cannot see; Spicer, who fears the police, but not God; Cubbitt, who dares not show his romantic feelings, which he covers by brashness. The character in the novel who resembles Ida most is Colleoni, the rival gang leader, who seems to own the whole visible and tawdry world-from cash registers and prostitutes to policemen.

Pinkie and Rose are in fact alienated figure in this world of Ida and Colleoni, which glitters with lust and self-gratification. They are strangers to the bright lights of Brighton and seem to belong more naturally in the world of darkness, the world of the murdered reporter, Hale, and the depraved Drewitt. Note how Hale, when trying to escape from Pinkie's gang, conjures up reminiscences of his childhood days, when he would find solace in secret, dark places. It is also interesting that when Drewitt dwells on his ruined marriage, he remembers Mephistopheles' reply to Faustus when asked where Hell is: "Why this is hell, nor are we out of it." Greene cleverly implies, however, that Brighton's Heaven - the bright, gleaming world of Ida and Colleoni-is a cheap and unappealing place; Brighton's Hell - the world of Pinkie-is at least authentic and not covered with the gloss of hypocrisy.

Pinkie and Hell

As Francis L. Kunkel says in The Labyrinthine Ways of Graham Greene, "Dante merely visited hell; Pinkie comes from there." He is literally a hellish figure, someone who represents the Devil, and who fights for a totally diabolical cause. The **climax** of his satanic career, for example, is his tempting Rose to kill herself, thus exploiting her love for him. Although unsuccessful, it demonstrates his malevolence in the guise of love, making him an ambassador of evil as totally dedicated to his cause as is a saint to the love of God. Even he is fascinated by his own diabolism, particularly when he ponders his forthcoming fake marriage to Rose and the state of mortal sin into which they will automatically be plunged. Greene has Pinkie see the murders of Hale and Spicer as only preludes to the total corruption on the edge of which he now stands.

Pinkie and Rebellion

T. S. Eliot, in his essay on Baudelaire, says that "The worst that can be said of most of our malefactors, from statesmen to thieves, is that they are not men enough to be damned." This cannot really apply to Pinkie, however, who virtually gloats in his conscious capacity for evil. His mock-chant to his belief in "one Satan" shows that he cannot possibly conceive of eternity, except in term of agony. Greene makes this more evident by his physical description of Pinkie, whose slate-like eyes are filled with the obliterating eternity he comes from and toward which he is moving. Pinkie, of course, has not been untouched by goodness or love. His childhood religious experiences and his attachment to Rose demonstrate that. But whenever this happens, he feels compelled to destroy it or soil it. On one occasion only is Pinkie overwhelmed by the possibility and reality of goodness and salvation. When he comes upon an old woman saying the rosary in an alley, he has the realization that redemption is possible, even in the most abject and apparently hopeless circumstances.

Pinkie and Puritanism

In his essay on Frederick Rolfe in *The Lost Childhood*, Greene says that "the greatest saints have been men with more than a normal capacity for evil, and the most vicious men have sometimes narrowly evaded sanctity." Greene evidently depicts Pinkie in this way, for we have the impression that the young gangster has the potential to be a great saint instead of a great sinner. It is noteworthy that Pinkie vowed, as a child, that he would be a priest, destined to save souls rather than destroy them. For Pinkie, Hell is a tangible concept, while Heaven is an intangible one. He finds he can trust Hell because he can live in it and control it in a sense, whereas Heaven is but a word to him. Pinkie succumbs to evil totally, yet this is accompanied by a strange form of puritanism worthy of comment.

His sexuality is unwanted, and he has what has recently been termed the "existential loathing of the flesh." Pinkie's impotence forces him to find sexual relief in acts of sadism, which calm the torment that rages within him. His passionate outbursts take the form of inflicting pain with such weapons as razor blades and "school dividers" (compasses). Pinkie wants to hurt Rose physically and make her scream instead of kissing her. He finds sensual pleasure in crushing a moth under his shoe, for example. The fact that he had to witness sexual activities when he was young suggests one reason why he does not wish to become engaged. It also suggests why he is so puritanical, in that he abstains from such pleasures as cigarettes, dancing, gambling and, of course, girls. His terror of the sexual act seems to spring from what Greene refers to as a horrible, unnatural pride. Lack of sexual desire would make marriage unthinkable, were it not for his desire to use it as an escape from the law. His attempted intercourse with Sylvie is particularly pathetic, since it is a deliberate effort to become used to women, and the disgust he feels at the act, making him say he would rather hang than marry, is indicative of the deeprooted problem he harbors.

Pinkie as a Dostoevsky Figure

Pinkie has been described as being the most Dostoevsky-like of all Greene's characters. For example, he indulges in a passionately violent revolt against God, and suicide holds a morbid fascination for him. He has been compared to Stavrogin, Kirillov and Stepanovitch, all of whom have violent, destructive quarrels with God. The murder of Hale may well be equated with Raskolnikov's murder of the old pawnbroker, in that they both wish to prove themselves above and beyond the natural course of law. They are also similar because both end up in isolation and alienation. It is noteworthy that both Raskolnikov and Pinkie turn to girls-Sonia and Rose-for some measure of light for the darkness in which they find themselves.

Theme of Brighton Rock

In this novel Greene pulls together his ideas on the "pursuit" motif, his concept of betrayal, his views on corrupted innocence, and his use of symbols to depict evil to convey one central **theme**: the religion of his main characters. Greene defines good and evil by portraying the characters of Pinkie and Rose, while employing such traditional **conventions** as the chase, coincidence, betrayal, and confession. The novelist uses all the tawdry jargon of the day to outline the equally cheap world of bookmakers, race-track gangs, and razor slashers who constitute the underworld of Brighton. Greene's use of setting is interesting, for by placing the bright lights of dance halls and pavilions beside the sea, he is at once capturing the ephemeral but recurring cheapness of human existence and the immutable continuity of the ever-changing and ever-lasting sea. On the surface, of course, the novel could be taken as another thriller, with Ida seeking justice, Pinkie personifying the bad element, and Rose providing the romance. All these elements are magnificently integrated to lend weight to the religious aspects of the main **theme**. And this main **theme** is dominated by the eternal presence of the Church, always apparent in its relentless pursuit of those who have made a commitment to it. This religious framework in fact lends allegorical meaning to *Brighton Rock's* central **theme**, which is that of justice in the form of right superseding wrong, and good overcoming evil.

Symbolism and Ida

Throughout the novel, Ida is continually described in terms of being a mother. Even Fred sees her as this, despite his rebellion against associating with her. She introduces herself to the mob at one point as Rose's mother. Yet we should really interpret all this in the wider sense of her representing humanity. Although she has a sense of right and wrong, she feels uneasy when faced with these clear-cut categories. Vital and strong, she believes that only what she sees around her is in fact real. Ida is in a sense the symbol of life as opposed to the death she forces upon Pinkie. Her whole attitude to avenging Fred's death is based on a primal sense of justice and a feeling for humanity. Her belief is in the "natural order" as opposed to a belief in God as such. Paradoxically enough, however, her conception of justice is much more simple than that which she thinks is inherent in the Christian conception. For right and wrong, as concepts in God's justice, are closely linked to good and evil, which are not facile concepts by any means. From another angle, Ida's actions represent a battle between the faith of humanity and the cult of power as outlined by Kite's mob.

The Characters and Catholicism

Pinkie and Rose have one thing in common - their Roman Catholicism. Although Rose is from Nelson Place and knows the symbols of evil as well as Pinkie, her innocence has not been corrupted by them. The good in her corresponds to the evil in Pinkie, and what is most evil in him needs her, since it cannot get along without goodness. He forces his corruption upon her by marrying her to keep her from testifying, and theirs becomes quite literally a marriage between Heaven and Hell.

Both characters establish the polarities of good and evil. Ida represents the via media, and therefore sees how alien Rose and Pinkie's worlds are to her view of mankind. Ida flounders when confronted with extreme goodness and extreme evil. She does not even have the vocabulary to meet their demands. Such concepts as God's mercy are beyond her comprehension, and she cannot deal properly with the spiritual drama being enacted before her. Pinkie, on the other hand, is totally dedicated to the forces of evil and directs all his energy toward fulfilling that dedication. To Pinkie, peace and satanic power go hand in hand- his two constant **refrains** are "Credo in unum Satanum" and "Dona eis pacem." The conflict lies in his Catholicism, which teaches him that every step he takes in the fulfillment of his creed is another step toward perdition.

| Brighton Rock and Baudelaire

It has been said that there is a strong touch of "Baudelairian Satanism" buried deep in Pinkie's soul, and in this respect one should turn to Morton D. Zabel's essay on Greene for some illuminating insights into what this means. He draws a connection between *Brighton Rock* and Eliot's essay on Baudelaire. Eliot, in discussing Baudelaire, says that the French poet assumed a strange dignity in the propagation of his sins, since his personal life was so sterile. The essay states that for Baudelaire, even damnation itself was "an immediate form of salvation... because it at least gives some significance to living." Eliot might well have been talking about Pinkie. There is certainly an identity achieved in the Baudelairian concept of Christianity, an identity achieved by the recognition of "moral Good and Evil" which are not natural Good and Bad or puritan Right and Wrong. According to Eliot, Baudelaire was at least able to appreciate the power of doing evil by "having an imperfect vague romantic conception of Good."

Pinkie's position of recognizing sin as being something exalted and of damnation being "an immediate form of salvation" has the same psychotic and perverted structure. No matter how we look at it, Pinkie's fierce attempt at self-identification is really an attempt to rise above the level of the animal by acknowledging Good and Evil. His total commitment to evil can be attributed greatly to the nature of his environment, which made it virtually impossible for him to have even "an imperfect vague romantic conception of Good." To him Heaven is something unknowable and unattainable that lies on the other side of death. The goodness which represents heaven on earth has been swamped by such memories as the Saturday night sexual activities of his parents, the horrors of his school life, and, of course, the instructions in crime given by the murdered

Kite. For Pinkie, the only tangible and palpable evidences of the spiritual life available to him lie in the underworld of Brighton, and they point inevitably to evil and damnation. The spiritual view is perverted and limited, but at least it allows Pinkie to seek and realize some form of human identity. The very fact of his being able to achieve even damnation is surrounded by the same kind of strange glory that surrounded Baudelaire, according to Eliot's interpretation.

Pinkie's Malevolence

It cannot be denied that Pinkie is a totally malevolent figure, but we should not be tempted to dismiss this by making him the innocent victim of slum conditions. To do that would be to restrict interpretations of the novel to a sociological level by omitting its all-encompassing spiritual dimensions. As a matter of fact, such an interpretation would fall down immediately by our pointing to Rose, whose innocence and goodness came out of the same slum conditions. The reasons for Pinkie's driving compulsion toward evil must be sought in the psychological and spiritual realms as well as in the environmental. Herbert Rittaber, in his essay, *The Two Worlds of Graham Greene*, calls Pinkie "at once the most dreadful and Satanic character in modern fiction." This claim is probably quite justified, since Pinkie has a unique, intuitive knowledge of the nature of evil. He demonstrates that knowledge by marrying Rose, since absolute evil demands more than a complete dedication to corruption-it demands the corrupting of that which is good. Pinkie seems to be banished from goodness, yet it is an ever-present reality before him in the form of Church ritual and in Rose's innocent and childlike faith. It is noteworthy, for example, that Pinkie is moved by music which reminds him of his choir-boy experiences and speaks to him in words of a love and beauty that are now lost to him.

The Novel and The Sacraments

Catholicism and its rites-including its music-continually affect Pinkie's thinking and actions, even though unconsciously. To fulfill himself, he has really to perfect his evil and assure his own damnation, and to do that he must attempt to obliterate the last remaining traces of his religious background. In a subtle way, Greene has used the seven sections of *Brighton Rock* to describe the process whereby Pinkie attempts to debase and dishonor the seven sacraments of the Church. The Sacrament of Holy Communion, for example, which ensures the strengthening of faith through the symbolic reception of Christ's body and blood, is perverted in a particularly repulsive way in Part Two. Pinkie's faith in evil is strengthened by his conviction that violence is absolutely necessary for his perverted salvation. He reinforces this belief by slashing Brewer, the bookmaker, with a razor blade. Coming into conflict with the police and Colleoni as a result of this encounter, he must justify his position of power in the jungle of Brighton. The grotesque **parody** of grace he has received by shedding blood gives him the nervous strength to display his belief in violence.

In Part Three, a vicious perversion of the Sacrament of Baptism takes place. Contrary to what is expected, Pinkie's baptism as a child has prepared him for a life of total commitment to sin. Regarding sex, his earliest knowledge was of the sordid and squalid relations between his mother and father, which resulted in an inverted and morbid puritanism on his part. Watching Rose in Part Three, he becomes momentarily aroused sexually, but this is immediately swallowed by his sense of ruthlessly imposed virginity. He feels trapped by his inability to fulfill what is expected of him sexually and realizes that again there is no escape except into the dark world of murder and corruption.

The Sacrament of Holy Orders is parodied savagely in Part Five, when Pinkie perverts the traditional renunciation of worldly pleasures by attempting to renounce the strange form of puritanism which circumstances have forced upon him. When he drinks the liquor, he finds it odious, however, and has a feeling of revulsion when he touches Spicer's ex-mistress. The reason for Pinkie's failure in this attempted excursion into the cheap world of Brighton lies not in his inability to indulge in cheap activities, but in the fact that they are merely cheap - not evil, which is necessary for Pinkie. At this point in the story the extent of Pinkie's corruption is shown by his determination to marry Rose in order to corrupt her.

The Sacrament of Marriage is debased in the Sixth Part by the wedding ceremony and the consummation, for Pinkie and Rose are locked in evil corruption rather than in Holy Matrimony. In the last part, Pinkie's desperate hopes for last-minute salvation are constantly balked and he fails to find mercy, at least on earth. The final unction given him as part of his last rites takes the form of vitriol in the face. He dies without contrition, in the terrible state of having tempted Rose to kill herself to drive her to her own damnation.

Structure of Brighton Rock

These few examples point to the fact that quite an elaborate and detailed analysis of the novel can be made on this allegorical basis. It is quite an astounding feat, from a structural point of view, in that the cruel parodying of the seven sacraments adds impact to the novel's emotional intensity. Other structural considerations come into play in the novel, all of which point to Greene's being a master of this art form. Studied from a dramatic point of view, for example, *Brighton Rock* displays all the power, pace, and passion of tragedy. From the murder of Hale to Pinkie's death we are taken on a frightening excursion leading to the inevitable conclusion, which has all the elements of tragedy. Herbert R. Haber says in fact that "Given Macbeth's conscience and social stature, Pinkie might almost be re-enacting that blood-drenched drama in modern dress." Furthermore, when studied in terms of spirituality, Pinkie's life and death actually can be seen as a modern re-enactment of Christ's Passion. We shall see how Greene reiterates this **theme**, particularly in *The Power and the Glory*, where many aspects of the whiskey priest's desperate odyssey to death resemble Christ's Passion also. In Brighton, Ida can even be seen as a Judas figure, just as the mestizo in the other novel. And Cubbitt's thrice-delivered denial of any connection with Pinkie has an obvious scriptural parallel in the Apostle Peter's three denials of knowledge of Christ.

Brighton Rock as an Entertainment

Graham Greene himself originally described *Brighton Rock* as an "entertainment," with which category we disagree wholeheartedly. Nevertheless, a few comments on this aspect of the novel might be worth making. The novel has, of course, all the trappings of a conventional thriller or detective story, and as such it can stand quite successfully. But note that there are two clear-cut story lines running through *Brighton Rock*. The first revolves around Ida's amateur but deadly pursuit of Pinkie in order to seek revenge, while the second deals with the psychological and religious complexities of the relationship between Pinkie and Rose. Beyond this, however, this dual story line is essential to the meaning of Greene's novel and his point of view. Notice how brilliantly the two story lines converge and clash whenever Ida converges with Pinkie and Rose. And while Pinkie is a diabolical figure, he is a spiritual one in the sense that Ida is not, with her "down-to-earth" view of mankind.

To Pinkie, Hell as a religious concept is very tangible to the extent that he touches it, manipulates it, and lives it, while the world of Brighton, though without pleasure for him, is not evil enough to be totally damned. To Ida, on the other hand, the thought of death is shocking and life is all-important, as we have seen. The fact that Ida cannot pity something she does not understand is testimony enough to her total divorce from the world of spiritual values to which Pinkie and Rose at least adhere, although poles apart.

Essential to the **theme** of *Brighton Rock* is this idea of the irreparable dichotomy between people whose lives are prompted by personally-devised philosophies, and people who are hurled into the obliterating effects of supernatural spirituality. When all Greene's major works are studied closely, it can be seen that this **theme** applies time and time again. *Brighton Rock* is a tale of good and evil, where the evil, personified by Pinkie, sets out to consume the good. It is a tale of Heaven and Hell, where the Heaven of Colleoni and Ida is the Hell of Pinkie, which he tries to dominate, but cannot. Pinkie belongs in no earthly world, not Kite's mob, nor Rose's, nor Ida's. His only home is the depths of the sea, which finally consumes his evil.

· ·

PLOT ANALYSIS

The central character in this novel is a whiskey priest who is unnamed, although he sometimes assumes the name "Montez." He lives in a small Mexican province, and has been a fugitive for eight years from the totalitarian, anti-religious regime which has taken over the province. Although he is an alcoholic and not in any way a good example of the priesthood, he still tries to continue his priestly duties by performing such rites as Mass and the baptism of children. The last priest in the province, he feels a sense of martyrdom, which he accepts without resolutely planning to escape. His main antagonist is a lieutenant of police, also nameless, who is like the priest in his zeal, but for the secular order. Born of peasant stock, the officer has a passion for reform, which he is willing to translate into action by killing, if necessary. An inner conflict is created by his encounter with the priest, who puzzles the lieutenant by espousing what to his State-oriented mind seems a lost and hopeless cause.

The priest's sense of guilt is compounded by his having committed adultery with Marcia, one of his parishioners in the town of Concepcion, where he last had a parish. He has a seven-year-old daughter, Brigida, and an interesting comparison is made between her attitude and her mother's toward the priest.

The girl is suspicious and scornful of the man who has made her an isolated figure, while the mother feels strangely proud that a priest has fathered her child. The hunted priest is gradually humbled by the fact that he is protected wherever he goes, and this is brought out in his relationships with a dentist, a trader, and a plantation owner who shelter him in turn in the course of his flight. The whiskey priest encounters another religious figure, Father Jose, a defrocked priest who has renounced his faith and is the victim of a shrewish wife, as well as of the mockery of his village. This priest shows no humanitarian feelings toward the whiskey priest, and even refuses to hear his confession, even though he has received permission to do so from the government.

The main conflict, which embraces a subtle and ironic interplay of moods and emotions, is between the whiskey priest and the lieutenant. The priest's attitude toward poverty, for example, is one that is ostensibly opposed to that of the lieutenant, although there is an implied meeting-point in both attitudes which are presented as two angles of vision. The lieutenant is in fact troubled by the methods used to capture and destroy the priest, namely, the taking and killing of hostages. An interesting juxtaposition is created here, for Greene very cleverly implies that the State needs dedicated, puritanical types like the lieutenant to survive, while the eternal values of God can survive in the tawdry, broken body of the whiskey priest. Neither figure is a free agent, for the lieutenant is bound by the written regulations of the State, while the priest is bound by the unwritten regulations of God. The priest's lack of freedom is shown by the fact that he allows himself to fall into a trap when he is summoned to deliver the last rites to an American gunman. The instrument of his betrayal is a mestizo, or half-breed, who is the Judas-figure in the novel. Recognizing the priest's identity when others do not, he waits his opportunity to pounce at the right time. Although he is a thoroughly contemptible figure, with the wheedling, ingratiating manner of a police informer, he is still drawn in a uniquely sympathetic light. His sinister manner is offset by the fact that he pleads for forgiveness after betraying the priest. At the end, the priest admits his weakness, cowardice, and lack of vision, but nevertheless goes to his death with the feeling that in some way he has fulfilled his function as a priest, despite all the evidence to the contrary. The reader has the distinct impression that the priest's execution has had some effect on the lieutenant, who is not as callously indifferent as he appears to be. This is one of Greene's most powerful and moving stories.

ANALYSIS OF CHARACTERS, THEMATIC MATERIAL, AND THEIR INTERRELATIONSHIPS

The Whiskey Priest-Motivation and Conflict

The priest in this novel is concerned with and is the object of two kinds of pursuit, one human and one divine. On a human level, he is the last priest in Tabasco, Southern Mexico, and as such is hunted by the Government, as personified by the lieutenant. He is an outlaw on two scores-he is a priest in a godless state and he has broken the laws of his Church, He is also a scapegoat, in that he fulfills his function as priest to the people until his betrayal and death, which makes his agony analogous to the Passion of Christ. On a **metaphysical** level he is also a divine scapegoat, because his pursuit by God transforms the locale "into the whole wasteland of original sin, the Priest into the human soul and the flight from the people into the flight of the soul from God" (James Newman, "The Divine Pursuit," *Juggler*, April 1947). The priest is in fact hunted to his own salvation. While the priest offers one kind of salvation, the lieutenant offers another in the form of a social heaven, achieved through material revolution devoid of spiritual content. The priest, on the other hand, offers the more intangible reward of eternal salvation through self-denial entailing a journey marked by frustration and pain. Yet, the conflict is not just the simple one of the world of Caesar versus the Kingdom of God. The lieutenant is in one sense a humanitarian who wishes to eliminate from the world of children all the social ills that made his own early life so wretched. He is also a frustrated character who cannot realize his ambition, since he has a realization that the world consists of dying human beings who apparently have a purposeless existence. Furthermore, his humanitarian instincts seem to be negated by his willingness to kill the innocent to make the world a happier place to live in. The priest is also a contradictory figure, for, although his kingdom is that of God, his own living has transgressed the laws of that kingdom, leaving him an abject figure, isolated from a society lost to him, but which he feels he can help save.

Structure of the Novel

This novel contains wide and rich dimensions unusual even for the best category of the Greene novel. Although the work is typically Greene - the priest is a characteristic Greene figure and the pursuit **theme** is familiar - it is unique because it contains two interwoven and interrelated structures which we will discuss later. We must not forget that *The Power and the Glory* is a modern symbolic novel and as such is bi-structural, in the sense meant by Edwin Muir when he said, "The main object of the one plot is to proceed by widening strokes, and to agree that it does so is to imply space as its dimension. The main object of the other is to trace a development, and a development equally implies time." (*The Structure of the Novel*, London, the

Hogarth Press, 1928.) This particular novel abounds in what Karl Patten calls "symbolic identifications," and the spatial development of this book depends on the cohesion of this series of identifications. The priest is at the hub of this, and all the other figures with whom he comes in contact are related to him symbolically in one way or another. We will go into these relationships in detail later.

Another unique aspect of this book is the fact that there is a strongly defined element of hope at the end. This hope is at the center of the religious **theme** of *The Power and the Glory*, which accentuates as it progresses the bond between the priest's life and that of Christ. This latter factor is essential to our appraisal of the work. The priest is betrayed by a Judas figure, whom he forgives; he goes to his death willingly and by way of altruistic self-sacrifice; he is, in a sense, "hung" beside a thief; and he dies for his faith in God. He is an extremely un-Christ-like figure, of course, in that his mission and life have been far from flawless. He has certainly dedicated his life to be an imitation of Christ's, but is painfully susceptible to human corruption. The dereliction of his death is certainly Christlike, however, in its noble aims, for although he has been unable to save mankind, he has redeemed himself and has borne witness to his faith in a world stripped of religious values.

The Priest, The Lieutenant, and Pinkie

The priest's immoral life stands in contrast to that of the lieutenant, in that the priest is an alcoholic and a fornicator, while the lieutenant is totally dedicated and puritanical. In this sense their roles are the reverse of what one might expect. Yet the priest can help his countrymen in the one way that the lieutenant cannot, namely by offering them solace and salvation through the administration of the Church's sacraments.

According to Church teachings, even the most sinful priest can be the means of granting God's grace to souls - the salvation of human beings does not depend on the sanctity of the priests who serve them. There is a distinct sterility in the brand of love for humanity as depicted in the lieutenant, as shown by his willingness to kill in cold blood. The essential difference between the priest and the lieutenant is eloquently expressed by the priest himself after his arrest, when he points out to his captor that totalitarianism depends on stringently disciplined men for survival, whereas God can swell and survive in the most wretched of humans.

Francis L. Kunkel has pointed out how Pinkie in *Brighton Rock* is a composite of the priest and the lieutenant. Both Pinkie and the priest are hounded to their death by ideologists hostile to them. As they plunge to their end, they carry their own hells with them, and are continually humiliated on the way. The priest accepts the humiliation, however, and achieves a form of martyrdom, while Pinkie rejects it and suffers wounded pride as a result. Still, the lieutenant and Pinkie resemble each other as well. They both feel betrayed and rejected by childhood, they both are alienated from God, and they are both virginal in an embittered way. Both are neurotically proud, lead ascetic lives, and share a passion for relentless destruction. By bringing the priest and the lieutenant into conflict, Greene in some ways synthesizes for us the complexities of Pinkie's character.

The Priest and Persecution

The Power and the Glory may well be considered a modern parable, spelled out in cruel and relentless terms, outlining the immutable and indestructible quality of religious faith. Yet the reverse would seem the case, since the priest's execution and the lieutenant's survival point ostensibly to the collapse of religion and the elevation of totalitarianism. The priest is but an agent of God, however, an imperfect, corrupt agent driven by a divine power into a human enactment of a highly emotional drama. The priest's death is in fact used by God, paradoxically enough, to demonstrate the eternal validity of religious belief by having it renewed in the person of the boy, Luis. The struggle between the priest's faith and the lieutenant's is thereby resolved by the boy's religious resurrection. The lieutenant has shown himself willing to destroy the Church itself to win the boy over, but his failure to do so shows the lack of appeal which totalitarianism has for the youth of the State. The new priest who arrives to carry on the dead priest's work put his trust in Luis, thus symbolizing the eternal renewal of religious faith.

The lieutenant's relentless persecution of the priest is worth studying, for his apparent hatred for the man turns out to be, really, a hatred for God. He unleashes his nihilistic hatred for God on the priest who seems to be the last remaining representative of divine justice (in the priest's terms) and of social injustice (in the lieutenant's). The priest is therefore at once a scapegoat of God, who literally uses him to further religious belief, and of the lieutenant, who sees in the priest the symbol of ecclesiastical corruption and an enemy of the State. The lieutenant's loathing for the priest is therefore both personal and impersonal, for the priest is the last tangible evidence of the Catholicism which the lieutenant sees as the source of all the social evils around him. The paradox is, of course, that both the priest and the lieutenant are aiming at the same thing, namely, the happiness of the human race. The fact that this aim is translated in diametrically opposed ways adds to the fascination of the human situation.

The Priest as a Scapegoat

The priest is a trapped figure. On two occasions he tries to find safety, but on both occasions he is called back to administer last rites to the dying. As Greene points out, he is like a tribal king who is also the slave of his people and dares not stop administering the sacraments, even if this means his dying in a condition of mortal sin. This use of the priest as scapegoat is not unique to Graham Greene, however. Bernanos, the French Catholic writer we discussed briefly earlier, has Pere Donissan, the priest in Sous le soleil de Satan, absorb the sins of a possessed girl in order to salvage her, and in Journal d'un cure de campagne, the young priest dies from and for the sins of his parishioners. Mauriac has the Abbe Alain Forcas take all the sins of his villagers upon himself, although he is the object of their contempt. It is interesting that Greene praises the works of both French writers in *The Lost Childhood*, and in his own priest depicts a scapegoat to show what he himself has described as the appalling mysteries of love existing in a ravaged world.

The whiskey priest in fact imitates the supreme scapegoat, Christ, by negating self for a sense of eternal responsibility. Mr. Kunkel, in his excellent study called *The Labyrinthine Ways of Graham Greene*, outlines the similarities between the events leading to the priest's execution and those leading to the death of Christ. The half-caste, for example, is Judas; Gethsemane is represented by the priest's agony in the cell; when the priest comforts the dying American murderer, he is Christ offering solace to the good thief; the lieutenant's wish to murder the priest rather than the American represents the mob's wish to kill Christ instead of Barabbas; and the cowardly Padre Jose's spurning of the priest is Peter's denial.

The Priest and Pursuit

The priest is an outlaw because he is a priest in a totalitarian regime, and his pursuit by man and God drives him to the supreme act of love, his own death on behalf of his fellows. God's pursuit has, of course, universal dimensions which the lieutenant's does not: God is after the soul and the world, while the lieutenant is after the priest and Tabasco. Greene therefore uses Tabasco in somewhat the same way he uses Scobie's colony, namely to represent a world corrupted by original sin and occupied by people inclined toward evil. The lieutenant's search for the priest can therefore also be seen as God's search for the soul of Everyman in that it is ruthless, relentless, and demanding. Greene has again chosen an ideal location for the enactment of this eternal drama, for Tabasco is virtually a hell-hole of corruption and decay.

Symbolically, vultures prowl the sky, hunting carrion, as they do also in *The Heart of the Matter*. Everything in the country reeks of decay, from the soul-destroying rain and hissing snakes to the relentless mosquitoes and crawling alligators. The inhabitants too are drawn deliberately to depict people at their most abject; the neurotic Mrs. Fellows with her dread of death; the starving children with their swollen bellies; the dentist with his broken-down implements; the defrocked priest living like a frightened rat; and, of course, the whiskey priest's illegitimate daughter decaying in her desperate sense of isolation. One can see, then, how the dual pursuit of the priest by secular and divine powers seems all the more terrifying and moving because of the abysmal setting in which it takes place. Tabasco is depicted as a place where all the forces of evil seem to have free play, and the power of God's grace as dispensed from the hands of a derelict priest is all the more awesome. It seems that there is no end to life or to death here, just as there is no end to the pursuit of man by man or by God. Although the priest's death is an end in one sense, it also symbolizes the endless and ever-recurring pursuit of man's soul by a power infinitely greater than the State.

The Priest and Sanctity

At times Greene creates a nightmarish atmosphere which is paradoxically designed to heighten the atmosphere of sanctity persistent in the novel. Two scenes come to mind which demonstrate this, one in the hotel room where the priest watches the wine he has purchased for Mass being consumed, and the other in the fetid and lust-filled prison cell. The first demonstrates the frightening depths of his faith, while the second shows that a strange, spiritual peace can be found even in the most horrible circumstances. Even in this apparently spiritual wilderness the priest finds continual evidence of the deep-rooted belief of the people in the fact that he is not betrayed to the police. This is particularly surprising, since there is a price on his head. Also a rare act of heroism on the part of Coral Fellows, who protects the priest at considerable risk, shows that faith in human nature can still exist even in Tabasco. This act is particularly moving in view of Coral's tawdry background and Brigida's scorn for her own father. Another event of significance to the priest is his stumbling by accident upon the Indian cemetery with its array of crosses. Referring to this particular passage, Francois Mauriac says, "We feel it is that hidden presence of God in an atheistic world, that subterranean flowing of grace which dazzles Graham Greene much more than the majestic facade which the temporal Church still erects above the peoples."

Greene makes powerful symbolic use of the priest's flight, for in it he captures the essence of a soul suffering without God.

The priest's final surrender of his soul to the love of God is found in the act of contrition he makes while he is awaiting death. It is here that his craving for sanctity is made fully evident, and made more poignant by his feeling of having done nothing at all for God. Thus, the whiskey priest, degraded and abject, meets his end having been pursued by two great powers, one temporal and the other spiritual. There is a sense, at the end, of an uncanny victory in his defeat.

The Priest and Interpersonal Relationships

As we have suggested earlier, a clear picture of the priest cannot be achieved fully unless we study the relationships of various characters to him. For the sake of convenience, we have separated these into six distinct categories.

A. The Dentist and the Priest

Tench, the English dentist stranded in the port town in which we find the priest, is modeled on an American dentist, Doc Winter, who is described by Greene in *Lawless Roads* as a man without hope and without God in the world. Tench, removed from a family he can barely remember, is like the priest in several respects. He is trapped in a country devoid of spiritual values. He wishes to escape, but cannot. He endures amidst the pain implied by his very profession. In the center of his apparent hopelessness, there is a tenacious desire to cling to life despite his terrible sense of isolation. It is ironical-consciously so on Greene's part-that we witness the priest's execution through his eyes as he is drilling the teeth of the police chief. The priest's death has an immediate effect on him, and his mood seems momentarily transformed into one of resolution as he decides to get out for good. Although we know somehow that he is trapped, at least we also know that the priest's execution had the effect of making Tench feel something for someone else's plight.

B. The Lieutenant and the Priest

As we have said, the lieutenant at first glance seems to have all the characteristics diametrically opposed to those of the priest. He has a passionate belief in social revolution, his world view is purely materialistic and economic, and he is violently anti-religious. Yet, at the same time he strongly represents one side of the priest's character and it would not be wrong to suggest that the two men are more alike than they are different. To begin with, they are both in a position of having dedicated their lives totally to a cause. The lieutenant has a deep, sincere regard for the welfare of the State's children, for whom he is willing to dedicate his life, if it would eradicate the suffering and deprivation he himself experienced in his childhood. Note how Greene openly verbalizes the similarity between the priest and the lieutenant by comparing the latter's room to a monk's cell and by stressing his ascetic celibacy.

The contrast between them-accentuated by the officer's cold efficiency and the priest's erratic behavior-is evened out by a clever reversal of positions at the end. For after the priest's capture, the lieutenant becomes confused and is put off guard by the priest's serene expressions of faith. He is also disturbed by the priest's calling him a good man for his charitable inclinations and his unabashed love for children. When we consider the lieutenant's devotion to his own "faith" in relation to Christ, we can see the meaning of Victor de Pange's observation: "The lieutenant is certainly not among the number of the damned. In trying to deny God he has learned to know him better." There is even a hint at the end of the book that the hard-hearted persecutor may well be on the edge of a revolutionary way of thinking.

C. Padre Jose, Juan, and the Priest

The whiskey priest's contacts with other priests is also worthy of study. Padre Jose, who has renounced his vows, married, and submitted to the will of the State, lives in a constant state of hopelessness and despair. Cut off from his divine function, he is filled with a dreadful sense of God amidst his sins and unhappiness. His relationship to the whiskey priest is of particular interest because the line separating the two is thin, but represents a great gulf. Although Padre Jose poses an ever present temptation to the whiskey priest, he never succumbs to it. The whiskey priest is indeed, in the most simplistic terms, a "bad priest," but he is nevertheless a priest to the very end.

On the other hand, another type of priest confronts the fugitive as an example of the traditionally accepted, "pious" type of martyr. This is Juan, whose life story is read aloud by the mother to her three children. Greene makes superbly ironical use of this situation to lampoon mildly the sanctimonious type of prose used to adulate such martyrs. Note too how the story of Juan shows him to have had something unreal and inhuman about his charity-he comes through as being "too good to be true." The whiskey priest, on the other hand, is a martyr of a different stamp; scuttling through back alleys, furtive and fearful, he is imbued with a sense of personal unworthiness. But without stressing the point. Greene makes him much more real and credible than Juan who is surrounded by a "plaster-saint" aura.

Judas and the Priest

The Judas figure in *The Power and the Glory* is the yellow-fanged mestizo whom the whiskey priest knows as a traitor early in the book. The priest also knows, as Christ knew, that this man is leading him into a trap that will destroy him. The reader must recognize the fact, however, that the whiskey priest crosses the border to his death not just to console the dying American, but because he knows in his heart that God is pursuing him and does not want him to escape. The priest's love for the mestizo is noteworthy in that he recognizes him as a poor creature for whom Christ also died, someone who is damning himself for so little. Yet there is a subtle similarity between the priest and the mestizo, for the priest is also a betrayer. He has betrayed the sacred trust of his priestly role by having abandoned many of his sacerdotal duties, by alcoholism, and by fornication. This form of treachery gives him the feeling that he is going to God stripped of everything. We may have a different picture of him, but at least that is how he himself feels-that he has been a Judas figure on a much wider scale than the mestizo.

Children and the Priest

Despite the difference between Coral Fellows and the priest's daughter Brigida which we noted earlier, there is one great element of similarity in them which is ultimately the same quality we feel in the priest-innocence. Both Coral and Brigida retain a strange innocence, despite their morbid maturity in the midst of corruption. It corresponds to the priest's innocence in its primal nature, and in the mysterious way such a quality can survive and sometimes even overcome the corruption that surrounds it.

The American and the Priest

The final character with whom the priest identifies is the American gangster, who, like the priest, is a fugitive. Greene makes subtle use of symbolism with this figure, by having his photograph hung next to the priest's in the police station, thereby suggesting the Crucifixion. The fact that the photograph with the priest is that of a first Communion party also has symbolic significance. Note that when the priest attempts to make the dying criminal repent, the gunman tries to persuade the priest to shoot his way out of the trap, just as Christ was urged by the thief to escape the Crucifixion. We can see, then, how the main figures associated with the priest mirror him in many ways, and how he in turn mirrors Christ.

Two Structures of the Novel

There are two structures operating in *The Power and the Glory*, one temporal and dramatic, and the other spatial and symbolic. Greene creates a subtle fusion of the two dimensions, a literary and aesthetic **convention** not uncommon in the modern novel. Dostoevsky, James, and Faulkner use the same device of combining space and time for dramatic effect. Aristotle first pointed out the necessity for significant and probably temporal action to make drama valid and dynamic. The modern novel has taken over this demand and blended it with the allusive methods of modern poetry in order to be able to deal with states of mind as well as positive physical action. In relation to Greene's novels, Joseph Frank's views on the similarity between primitive art and modern art are appropriate ("Spatial Form in Modern Literature" in *Criticism: The Foundations of Modern*

Literary Judgement). Frank relates these art forms to the "world as a realm of evil and imperfection." Since original sin is at the heart of Greene's Catholic metaphysics, his employment of temporal and spatial structure satisfies Frank's views that artists dealing with this type of world should "create aesthetic forms that will satisfy the spiritual needs of their creators" and, of course, of the audience these creators address.

The Priest and Everyman

The whiskey priest, with his indecisions, cowardice, irresponsibility, and underlying moral strength, is the modern prototype of the mediaeval concept of Everyman. Just as Everyman discards everything but Good Deeds, the priest goes to his death with nothing but his essential faith in God. Greene hammers this point home by having the priest lose or abandon such religious symbols as his chalice and breviary, until he has no possessions at all. Greene himself has said that "we are still within the period of the Morality," and that a tension must be maintained between that and the "play of characters," In *The Power and the Glory* he gives us a temporal character study of the whiskey priest that is dramatic, and places it in a spatial form that is symbolic. His structure is therefore closely allied to that of allegory, although its complexities defy that simple category. The tension which holds his "morality play" and his "play of characters" together is maintained by the power inherent in Greene's creative drive. It is a remarkable achievement, for he has not only created one character out of many loose fragments, but has also succeeded in making him a tenacious man of God, despite his frailties and abject condition. The whiskey priest has, therefore, all the dimensions of a modern Everyman, while radiating a quality that extends beyond comprehension. For, by his uncanny use of temporal and spatial conventions, and by his allegorical inferences, Greene has also created a character who relates to Christ. The fact that we too can relate to him makes his achievement all the more remarkable.

THE HEART OF THE MATTER

....

PLOT ANALYSIS

The locale of this novel is a West African colony still under British control during the Second World War. The main character, Major Scobie - known as "Ticki" to his wife - is a police chief there, enjoying a reputation for honesty and integrity which make him an ostensibly outstanding figure in an environment marked by corruption and deceit. Scobie is a convert to Roman Catholicism, a position which makes him regard every conflict as a major moral issue. One of the resultant problems is his inability to make bold, definitive decisions without introducing the element of pity into his relationships. This is shown, for example, in his reaction to the news that he has not been chosen as district commissioner, for he feels pity for his wife more than for himself. His sensitive reactions to such situations are often unknown to others or are misunderstood by anyone but himself, leaving him more and more in a position of isolation and alienation.

This sense of isolation is not relieved by the character and disposition of his wife, Louise, who is a weak, pretentious woman, ambitious for her husband without appreciating his sensitivity or scrupulous sense of honor. She has been deeply affected by the loss of their only child some years earlier, and her childlike reliance on Scobie serves only to heighten his feelings of inadequacy. Her attitude has a detrimental effect on her husband's sense of integrity, for he compromises his ideals when she pressures him into raising the money to allow her to leave the colony for awhile. This compromise takes the form of borrowing money from Yusef, a wily, unscrupulous Syrian merchant and smuggler who, strangely enough, loves Scobie as a fellow human sufferer and yet despises him for his honesty. When Louise leaves the colony, Scobie's feelings of desperate loneliness drive him into an adulterous relationship with Helen Rolt, a young survivor from a ship that had been torpedoed by a German submarine.

Helen also succeeds in intensifying Scobie's isolation by pouring scorn on his religious scruples, which prevents his getting a divorce and remarrying. Her lack of comprehension makes Scobie's agony more acute when Louise, who has returned to the colony and suspects her husband's infidelity, invites him to receive Holy Communion with her at a forthcoming Sunday mass. Scobie fully recognizes the theological implications of his adultery, particularly when he cannot bring himself to guarantee in the confessional that he will completely break off relations with Helen. Again through a sense of pity for Louise, he profanes the sacred act of Communion by sharing it with his wife while he is in a state of mortal sin.

In Catholic terms, this sacrilegious Communion sets the seal on Scobie's damnation. To add to his dilemma, Scobie discovers that he is being "watched" officially by Wilson, a British counter-intelligence agent who has arrived in the colony to look into the smuggling of industrial diamonds to Nazi Germany. Wilson not only observes Scobie's underhanded dealings with Yusef, but also looks on Scobie contemptuously for the way he neglects his wife, Louise, with whom Wilson is in love. Scobie now finds himself trapped: his career is on the brink of ruin, his marriage is disastrously unhappy, he has reached an impasse in his relationship with Helen, and in theological terms he regards himself as facing eternal damnation. Feigning a serious heart condition, Scobie commits suicide as a final gesture of pity for those around him, whom he feels will be relieved by his death. He does this with the full knowledge of the possible damnation facing him. His wife's lack of insight is shown by her remarks to the priest, after Scobie's death, that her husband was a bad Catholic who could not love anyone. The priest, however, is more sympathetic to Scobie, recognizing in him a fellow-sinner obliged to choose the only path open to him according to his conscience. The priest feels sure that in spite of all he did, Scobie loved God, and leaves us with the impression that salvation is possible for Scobie.

ANALYSIS OF CHARACTERS, THEMATIC MATERIAL, AND THEIR INTERRELATIONSHIPS

Pity and Scobie

Before embarking on any detailed analysis of this novel, it is essential to examine the concept of "pity" as used by Greene in his depiction of the main character, Scobie. While the Oxford Universal Dictionary defines it as "a feeling of tenderness aroused by the suffering or misfortune of another, and prompting a desire for its relief," the word often carries with it an implication of contempt. Yet the pity which is essentially the key to Scobie's character is something more profound than that, being linked to the concept of love as defined by Berdyaev: "an eternal affirmation" of one's personality. In Scobie's case, however, there are so many negative manifestations of this pity-his self-deception, for example-that they eventually destroy him. If, then, the pity as displayed by Scobie is an emanation in some way of Catholicism, or at least of the effect that Catholic culture has had on him, we must examine Greene's vision of pity and its relationship to the Christian concept of love.

Christ told man to love. This does not imply that the quality of pity should be absent from the love given, but rather that a conceptual compassion for mankind should prompt men to act existentially toward each other creatively and selflessly. But when pity is isolated from this creative, selfless, and existential act of love, it becomes a negative quality, a bowing down to and identification with the misery it attempts to relieve, and ultimately can lead to nihilism and self-destruction. This in its roughest terms is what happens to Scobie. Greene does not mean Scobie to represent only an isolated example of what can result from displaying pity with the absence of love, however. In Greene's terms, this disastrous flaw assumes universal dimensions, since it epitomizes the collapse of Christendom and the dissolution of the Christian ideal of pity as an integral part of and as an engendering force behind the total demands of love.

In view of what have said, however, it would not be at all cynical to describe Scobie himself as a "pitiable" character, since he is, in the long run, himself the victim of the human weaknesses that make Christian demands for "total love" impossible to meet. These weaknesses manifest themselves in the misery he chooses to inhabit, in the decaying civilization he was born into, and, ultimately, in the consciously hopeless but strangely noble attempt he makes to translate the divine ethic of love into a human situation marked by corruption and corroded by decaying values. In short, Scobie cannot show the love demanded of him by the Christ who is at the center of his faith. All he can do is display pity divorced from that love as used in its widest sense, a love which makes demands beyond his capability and comprehension. In this sense he symbolizes the failure, not of Christianity, but of a humankind striving to love and finding itself balked by its own intrinsic faults.

Structure and Background

As a novel, *The Heart of the Matter* is a very carefully and intricately structured work, consisting of over fifty scenes which comprise its three books. Yet it is a comparatively short novel, and Greene is consciously adding an **epic** quality to the various stages of Scobie's disintegration by elaborating the form. The very locale of the novel, a small West African colony, sets an immediate tone of decay and corruption, intensified by use of physical symbols, such as a vulture that settles on a corrugated roof. The fact that it is wartime is also symbolic, for the war itself seems just another isolated example of the universal corruption that manifests itself in the colony's activities.

Innocence and decadence are at once personified respectively by the poetry-loving detective Wilson and the Scobie-hating colonial-type, Harris. Note how cleverly Greene introduces Scobie to the reader through the meeting of these two characters, denoting the clash and intermingling of innocence and decadence. The use of the rusty handcuffs and broken rosary is equally brilliant, being at once emblems of Scobie's profession and faith. Moreover, the fact that the handcuffs are rusty immediately points to the hopelessness and meaninglessness of Scobie's attempts to apply law to a population totally indifferent to its existence. Furthermore, the fact that his rosary is broken suggests the impossibility of Scobie's being able to fulfill the supernatural injunction to love - and especially to love his wife, Louise. The complicated concept of pity comes into play before, during, and after the scene in which Scobie breaks the news of his not being promoted. Greene's introduction of the vulture again is particularly potent, and there is a sudden hint that Louise is as loathsome to Scobie as is the carrion-eating fowl. So his pity seems tainted with contempt and might make Scobie appear contemptible were Greene not to woo, very subtly, a sense of infinite pity for Scobie himself from the reader.

The attraction Wilson finds toward Louise, Scobie's conversation with the smuggler Yusef, and the artificiality of colony life as depicted at the party all add to the general climate of corruption and decadence already established. It is the very fact that human nature, with all its propensities for decay, has not had time to conceal itself behind any mask that makes Scobie positively love the colony. There is, of course, the very pointed symbolism of the quayside scene, in which Scobie releases the gaseous native-medicine from the bottle, as if unwittingly allowing the spirit of evil to permeate the atmosphere and influence the inhabitants. Greene communicates an appalling sense of Scobie's desolation when he tells us that the police officer, sitting in the bathroom with his bleeding hand, a disturbed rat, and his "boy" Ali, has an uncanny sense of feeling at home. Yet, observe how this scene is immediately followed by the one in which Louise admits her hatred of the colony and her desire to go to South Africa. When she falls asleep clutching his finger after his painfully deliberate words of comfort, we feel again Greene's **theme** and Scobie's downfall-pity.

Symbols of Law and Corruption

Novels dealing with law in any form often contain strong symbols: Dickens' *Bleak House*, for example, has fog, and Kafka uses twilight in *The Trial*. Since Greene's novel deals-at least on its simplest level-with two types of law, temporal and supernatural, one would expect and does in fact receive, a plethora of symbolism to strengthen the **theme**. In one sense, Scobie himself is a most potent symbol of law and order in the colony. His relationship with Yusef alone demonstrates his reputation as being the one man in the colony who can be trusted, and he is thus set up on an external level as a model of integrity in the midst of corruption. Yet on a deeper, internal level, Scobie happens to be the most untrustworthy character in the work. Greene helps our growing awareness of this fact by his use of symbols.

We have already discussed his introduction of the vulture and the rat, and Greene makes it very clear that these loathsome creatures are very close to Scobie, and that they are not to be regarded merely as emblems of a rapacious and repugnant world devoid of love. He implies, for example, that to Scobie, his wife is both vulture and carrion, at once a creature bent on destruction and a decaying organism waiting to be devoured. Scobie's feeling of rapport with the rat and the broken-down trappings of the bathroom suggest that he feels at home only in a foul underworld that the most bestial humans in his colony would find repugnant. At this point our initial discussion on pity comes into play. By immersing his interior self in something akin to sub-human compassion, while maintaining the exterior applications of comfort for his wife and integrity to the colony, Scobie becomes much more suspect than the most flagrant thief in the colony.

Yet again Greene very cleverly and, in fact, very poignantly prevents our falling into the trap of despising Scobie as being a hypocrite. By having him destroy the Portuguese Captain's letter to his daughter, Greene makes him first of all a sympathetic figure, since his action is prompted by a sense of compassion.

But the novelist also makes us aware that this act has also helped Scobie along the path to his own damnation. To begin with, on the external level, he has broken the law, which until now he has represented so admirably. But on the deeper level, he has transgressed a much more profound law, inasmuch as his act was helped along by the fact that the Captain is a fellow Catholic and that Scobie's own daughter had died. Pity has therefore made him break the legal code and highlights the loss of his sense of inner integrity. Just as some policemen are bribed by money, Scobie has been bribed by something much more lethal-pity stripped of spiritual love. We have yet another forecast of impending disaster in his assurance to Louise that he will raise the money to send her to South Africa, despite the fact that he knows he cannot borrow the money. His capacity for pity is therefore reinforcing his knowledge that he has a concomitant capacity for damnation.

The Element of Despair

Greene does not allow the novel to become an inner spiritual dialogue between Scobie and his conscience. By introducing external action at the right moments, he not only provides necessary interludes-as in the scene when the vague, spying Wilson goes to the bedroom to look for the rat-but also ensures the mobility of the novel's action. He also ensures that this action bears down on Scobie, and this is particularly potent when Scobie has to reach Bamba, the jungle station where Pemberton has committed suicide. For it is here that the great theological **theme** of despair comes into play and is brought into bitingly sharp relief by Greene's use of symbolism. In his dream, for example, the friendly tongue of the green snake that touches his cheek is another reminder of the ultimate in Scobie's pity-his rapport with bestiality. Note too the Stygian description of the stream that he and Ali cross, a piece of symbolism at once chilling and ominous, since Scobie crosses the stream to face the Church as personified in Father Clay.

When Scobie conflicts with Father Clay directly on the question of whether Pemberton is damned or not, his annoyance at the priest's insistence on ritualistically quoting the Church's teaching on suicide is undoubtedly based on his own deep doubts. It is interesting too that Scobie's argument against the Church's teaching is centered on his hope in God's pity. Scobie is really in a position of having to equate divine mercy with his own brand of pity, and there seems to be a note of controlled but fearful panic in his protestations. The nightmares he has later, in which the dead Pemberton is replaced by both himself and Louise, are in themselves indications of the terrors he harbors.

Pemberton's suicide is of great significance to the novel, since it evokes in Scobie a profound and unanswerable dialogue on the question of whether Christ's death on the Cross can in fact be regarded as suicide. The fact that he later openly identifies Pemberton's self-destruction with Christ's immolation in itself shows that Scobie's pity, when taken to its ultimate, would - and in fact does - lead to and justify suicide not only in human, but also in divine terms. Furthermore, as Greene himself points out, Pemberton's death is linked in an obscure way with Scobie's attitude to Louise. When we remember the impact Pemberton's letter had on Scobie, it is noteworthy that the sight of Louise writing a letter prompts him to damn himself even further by borrowing her passage money from Yusef. Her departure to the sound of the vultures on the roof further hammers home the destructive quality of Scobie's pity. This lethal pity is even demonstrated to Wilson, for when Scobie lies to him that Louise has sent her love, he is at once condoning his wife's possible adultery, encouraging Wilson's infatuation, and intensifying his own isolation. We must not neglect the fact that in telling Wilson this lie, Scobie is also revealing the cruel aspect of his pity.

Scobie and Helen

We discussed how Greene uses external action in the form of Pemberton's suicide both to keep the novel mobile and to add external impact to the doom that is engulfing Scobie. By introducing Helen Rolt as a survivor of a wrecked ship, he does the same thing again with, however, a complete reversal of intention regarding the symbolism. The fact that a river is involved shows a similarity to the journey to Bamba, but the river that brings Helen to Scobie has a lifegiving quality about it. There is even the suggestion of a newborn child in Greene's description of the unconscious girl. So in Pemberton and Helen we have symbolized for us the ultimate extremes of human existence, both of which combine with strange **irony** to seal Scobie's fate.

The scene in which the young child dies is worthy of close study, because here, for the first time, we sense Scobie's identification with Christ Note that the phrase "the heart of the matter" is used in this scene, for Scobie, while feeling utterly isolated in his omnipotent sense of pity for suffering humanity, questions the limits to which pity can lead one. But, even the idea that Helen's revival represents in some way a resurrection from the dead is counteracted by the death-like atmosphere that brings her and Scobie together; the conversation which triggers off their relationship concerns Scobie's dead child and Helen's dead husband. From the point of view of Scobie's position as a Catholic, his statement about one's responsibility to the dead is startling. By stating that we have no responsibility toward someone once that person is dead he directly countermands

Church teachings on the efficacy of prayers for the souls of the departed. But it is less startling when we recollect Scobie's argument with the priest. Here again he is perhaps indulging in some highly subjective theological wishful thinking, relying with an air of quiet desperation on the pity of God.

The destructive aspects of Scobie's pity are now translated into sexual terms, and in Greene's very use of the word "promiscuity" there is a strong flavor of Scobie's lusting after his devouring sense of pity. It is almost as if Scobie's apprenticeship in the bitter trade of pity has now ended and a new phase in his career of self-annihilation has begun. Greene is careful to remove any hint of joy, even on a purely neural level, from this scene. Scobie's act is again one prompted by pity; pity for him spells destruction; his sexual activity with Helen is automatically shrouded in disaster. Even Scobie's own symbolical vision of Helen is clouded with despair, for the girl he once saw as a child now lies beside him like cannon-fodder. When the scene ends with the cocks crowing in the distance, we sense that the new day they herald is in fact the dawn of Scobie's total destruction.

Guilt, Pity, and Responsibility

Scobie's feelings of responsibility to Helen spring from his consuming pity and are encased in guilt. These are intensified by the incestuous aspect of Scobie's adultery hinted at by Greene's accentuating Helen's childlike quality, symbolized mainly by the stamp album, and by his equating Scobie's emotions toward her with those of his own dead daughter. Greene's depiction of the whole adultery scene has been severely criticized, mainly on three counts. First, it is "heavy" to the point of being positively dolorous. Second, the explanation of the adultery, based on pity and from which lust is apparently absent, seems almost too contrived and overdone. Finally, the reader is sometimes puzzled as to the extent of Greene's "intrusion" as a narrator into the world of Scobie's emotions.

Greene's champions on these charges, however, would argue that to begin with, he is in fact dealing with a lugubrious human situation and would be unfaithful to the general climate of the book were he to underplay the tragedy. Moreover, Greene carefully notes that it is Scobie's body that has lost its sense of lust, but does not himself say that lust is totally absent. Finally, the novelist is justified in leaving certain aspects of Scobie's character deliberately mysterious, since it is not his function in this novel to delve into his character's psychology. At one point Greene in fact does reveal certain conflicting elements in Scobie's personality by exposing them vicariously in the shallow characters of Wilson and Harris. There is the melancholy, oppressive lust that lures Wilson into the brothel, for example, and the almost whining tone of self-pity that dominates his attitudes. Harris, on the other hand, has those corrosive elements of self-disgust, morbid nostalgia, and sense of rapport with reptiles that seem to be the traditional trappings of the worst features of colonial decadence. Greene is showing here that Scobie's unhappiness is unique in the depths, complexities, and tormented religiosity of its ingredients. The end result, however, namely loneliness, is ingrained in the death-like life of the colony.

The complications caused by Helen's insistent nagging, their quarrel, and Father Rank's visit all serve to intensify our awareness of Scobie's mounting despair. His statement in the letter to Helen, for example, that he feels he loves her more than he does God is one he makes without knowing why. Even the quarrel serves only to intensify his pity for and responsibility toward Helen. The priest's visit prompts one of the crucial and, for Scobie, unanswerable questions of the novel: how can one possibly love God if by so doing one of God's creatures must suffer? Again, his pity for Helen and Louise drives him deeper into the mire of human corruption by his helping the smuggler Yusef. Scobie, who has earlier claimed that he is the only unpitiable character in the world, now begins to wonder if even he is pitied, even by such totally corrupt people as Yusef and the Captain.

Religion and Suicide

Scobie's suicidal thoughts are, from their first introduction into the novel, inextricably bound with his belief that Christ killed himself. With Louise's return, Greene introduces more symbols denoting the depth of Scobie's despair and the inevitability of his total self-destruction. The picture of his dead daughter, and the description of the mosquito net as being grey ectoplasm, give the reader the feeling that Scobie sees himself surrounded by reminders of the impending disaster. Louise's testing him by inviting him to receive Communion with her and Helen's scornful ignorance of what this means to a Catholic place Scobie in his final dilemma. The sense of exile engulfing him reaches its peak when he feels that he is completely abandoned by his inability to join the others in receiving the redeeming sacrament. Pity again traps him, since his being absolved from his state of mortal sin would necessitate going to confession, which in turn would mean his total break from Helen. His pity for the state of abandonment she would be in is equalled only by his pity for the wife he has betrayed.

Greene introduces a strange note of theological symbolism into the scene in which Wilson, bleeding on the floor after Louise has struck him, becomes for a split second a pathetic

Christ figure. In his tacit abjection he even seems to offer some kind of momentary redemption for Scobie. Yet even when Scobie damns himself and desecrates God by receiving a sacrilegious Communion, Greene is really posing three questions. Is Scobie damning himself through love for others? If so, would not a merciful God forgive someone who has thus sacrificed himself, thus obliterating the self-damnation? And finally, is Scobie's act one of love or of pity in its most debased connotations?

Scobie's suicide plans seem almost incidental now compared to the outer manifestations of his inner moral collapse. The fact that Yusef really loves him in itself seems to indicate that any form of love in Scobie's world can coexist only with complete corruption. His growing distrust of Ali, leading to the servant's death, suggests to us that Scobie by now cannot help destroying everything he touches. Yet Greene consciously introduces a note of ambiguity here, suggesting at once Scobie's innocence, in that his only guilt here lies in having distrusted Ali, and his guilt, since his act was prompted by a self-pity devoid of compassion for others. Note that immediately before the suicide, we are presented with a picture of a Scobie who is both innocent and guilty. His ultimate pity for God when he is at the point of death is almost inevitable, for in Scobie's dying moments he sees all his deeds as having been aimed at defying the Supreme Being. In Scobie's theology of pity, God should be the highest object of the emotion that drives him to suicide. The final dialogue between Louise and Father Rank is probably the only elegy possible for Scobie. For when the priest says he believed Scobie loved God and Louise answers that he loved no one else, she undoubtedly strikes at the true heart of the matter.

The Concept of Love

If we state that Scobie's life and death is an attempt to imitate the life and death of Christ, a further examination must be made of the idea of pity in relationship to the concept of love. For in Catholic theological terms, Christ's death on the Cross is the ultimate act of love, an act of divine immolation for the salvation of mankind. Translated into the human dimensions within which Scobie operates, this reveals itself as his anguished and misguided efforts to fulfill an attitude of salvific responsibility toward the human beings he sees around him. He sees his fellow creatures as fellow victims and his blundering attempts to help them as acts of pity. Yet it is a tale of tragic contradictions, since his actions lead progressively toward disaster, despair, and finally suicide. It might be more accurate to say, therefore, that Scobie's "fault," if we can call it that, lies in confusing human pity with divine love, and in trying to be rather than to imitate Christ.

When we look as dispassionately as we can at Scobie's actions, however, it is difficult to equate them with anything approaching human pity, far less divine love. Adultery, breaking the legal code, consorting with smugglers, a possible assistance in the murder of Ali, deliberate sacrilege, and carefully planned suicide would on face value, hardly add up to good Catholic action motivated by pity. Needless to say, we cannot judge the deeds of a personality so complex as Scobie's on face value only. The most we can say is that a great deal of Scobie's activity, disastrous as it turns out to be, is motivated by a genuine attempt to lessen the sufferings of others. His adulterous relationship with Helen, however, is hard to justify as an act of pity, and Greene comes dangerously close to being absurd in his attempt to make us understand this relationship in terms of such pity.

From the point of view of Scobie's position as a Catholic, many of his transgressions would have to be placed in the category of mortal sin, since he has a full knowledge of what his actions mean in terms of his own damnation. As a Roman Catholic who believes in the rules of the Church, he commits sins deliberately, consciously, and with total awareness of the fact that, according to ecclesiastical teachings, he is thus spelling out his own damnation. We must remember that final, brief conversation between the priest and Louise. Scobie undoubtedly did love God with a love which comes through, at best, as warped compassion for others and, at worst, as abject self-pity. It also seems clear that he finds it virtually impossible to love anyone, even in the most elementary expression of that emotion. These factors, coupled with his final renunciation of the world, seem to point to Scobie's being a man so deeply disturbed psychologically that his actions at times border on the insane. Greene did not set out to outline Scobie's life and death in these terms, however, and for our purposes we must concentrate on the theological aspects of his actions and their results.

Immaturity of Scobie's Faith

Everything about Scobie suggests immaturity-his human relationships, his version of pity and his attitude to religion. He seems to be able to function only on a child-like level, and even his initial depiction of the trustworthy policeman symbolizing integrity amidst corruption has a "toy soldier" atmosphere about it. The only way Scobie can build up his own image of himself to himself and to others is to place everyone and everything around him in a child-like context, closely approaching fantasy. Greene brings this out in many ways: Scobie's retreating into his own little world in the bathroom, his view of Helen as a little girl, his regarding the natives of the colony as his children, and the reiterated image of his dead daughter. In this respect, then, we see his pity in a new light, namely as a safe hideaway from the grown-up world where he would have to face up to his responsibility as a man. His vision of pity and responsibility are closely linked to his vision of Catholicism - and both visions are blurred by his essential immaturity.

We mentioned earlier the concept of Christian love as being a "creative, selfless, and existential act." Since Scobie functions on such an immature level, however, his pity and the responsibility that springs from it must lead to disaster, since the real world Scobie inhabits does not operate on terms of childlike fantasy. Scobie's religious belief is based on immature pity which, on his immature level, he equates with mature love. Note, for example, how Pemberton's youth has such an effect on Scobie, leading him to argue with the priest that God must surely pity the young. His attitude of course leads to a frenetic attempt on Scobie's part to seek maturity by reducing everything-including God-to immature proportions. His Catholicism is in fact a child's catechism desperately trying to come to terms with an essentially cynical, adult, and non-religious world.

Seen in this light, then, we cannot help but have a more sympathetic attitude toward Scobie than we might otherwise. In Catholic theological terms, as we have said, he is totally responsible for the actions he perpetrates in direct defiance of God's laws as outlined by the Church. But in human and, we might even dare to say, psychological terms, he is innocent, and what damns him from the very beginning is not his transgression of God's will, but rather the crippling tension continually generated by his retrogression into a childhood world, while simultaneously attempting to progress in a world corrupted by adult indifference to decent values. In the dead bodies of the two boys, Pemberton and Ali, Scobie in fact sees himself, or rather foresees the fate which he, a middle-aged man, must necessarily bring upon himself. Scobie's faith can be defined as a disastrous attempt to mature spiritually by imposing spiritual immaturity upon the world which rejects and finally destroys him.

Scobie, Society, and Christendom

So far we have talked at length about Scobie's relationship to Christianity; that is to say, his attitude to the Christian ethic and his position as a member of the ecclesiastical structure known as the Roman Catholic Church. What is worth examining briefly, however, is his position as a product of the social, historical phenomenon known as Christendom. It is interesting that Greene, himself a man of astute social awareness, seems to be almost totally unconcerned with the social ills, the ethnic clashes, or the class distinctions that obviously must affect the life of Scobie's colony. Greene is merely using this locale as the stage for a highly personal tragic story of one man's disintegration. Yet Scobie is also a symbol of both a decaying imperialist class system and a decayed theological social structure. Scobie is very much a product of Western Civilization.

As we mentioned before, his attitude to the natives is one of father to children, and this is probably one of the psychological reasons for his loving the place. His imperialist uniform automatically makes him a father figure, an emblem of colonial paternalism of the worst kind. Scobie's Christian pity for the natives takes a negative form of accepting their corruption, their social malaise, their degradation. It is essential for him, with his immature personality and beliefs, to keep them that way. As an avowed Catholic, he has a moral responsibility to help the progress of the people of the colony. He fails. And if we see him as a symbol of both Imperialism and Christendom, we can see how the historical failure of these two great systems are mirrored in his very inactivity and dramatized in his total moral bankruptcy.

Greene makes this point very patently by accentuating the symbols of the rusty handcuffs, representing corroded Imperialism, and the broken rosary, representing collapsed Christendom. The corrupt sterile colony, with Scobie at its center, is in fact the graveyard of the faded and moribund values on which the whole of Western Civilization was founded and which lie at the heart of its decline. When we view Scobie from this angle, therefore, we can see his tragedy in historical dimensions. His failure as a police officer is in part due to the fact that he really believes in the laws of Imperialism, and his token gestures at enforcing these laws become all the more pathetic in the face of historical progress. Correspondingly, his failure as a Catholic is in part due to the fact that he is a survivor of Christendom, striving desperately to impose simply-defined moral values on a highly complex, immoral society. If we examine *The Heart of the Matter* from this perspective, we can see that it deals with the disintegration of a whole culture as well as the moral collapse of an individual.

CRITICAL COMMENTARY

. . . .

INTRODUCTION

There is a great deal of ambiguity surrounding the critical evaluations of Graham Greene's works. On the whole, it can safely be said that his works have not received the evaluation they deserve, and considerations of his position have fallen mainly into two groups. The first group tends to admire him to the point of adulation, almost elevating him to the rank of a religious prophet. The second group is divided into Catholic and secular schools of adverse criticism: the Catholic school concentrates on finding implications of heresy in his works and the secular school attacks him for adhering to an extremely orthodox and bizarre Catholic religion of his own making. There is a critical via media, however, and it is to this that we must turn to explore the most valid aspects of critical evaluations of his work. It should be said, however, that many problems remain untouched in studies of Greene's novels, and it is to be hoped that this defect will be remedied by future criticism.

Rather than make a bald list of works on Greene, it is more profitable to make an investigation of the various kinds of approaches that have been made to his writings. In the course of this survey we shall ignore some essays which, although devoted exclusively to Greene, are in fact valueless. On the other hand, we shall mention some critical studies in which Greene's works are only mentioned incidentally, but which are of great value in any appreciation of his literary stature.

SURVEY OF CRITICISM

Probably no contemporary writer has elicited such diverse criticisms as Graham Greene. He has been called a supreme artist and a hack, a Jansenist and an orthodox Catholic, a Sartrean existentialist and a literary Thomist. In a work called *This is Catholic fiction* (*Sheed and Ward*, 1948, p. 33), Sister Mariella Gable says that Greene "has expanded the boundaries of the English novel." Mary McCarthy, on the other hand, says that he has "produced a series of modern and highbrow novels under the formal discipline of Edgar Wallace and E. Phillips Oppenheim," and that he displays almost diabolical insincerity in so doing ("Graham Greene and the Intelligentsia," *Partisan Review*, XI, 1944, p. 228). Arthur Calder-Marshall calls the typical Greene character a "Greenelander," and Morton Dawson Zabel says that the average Greenelander "may work for evil or good, but it is his passion for moral identity that provides the nexus of values in a world that has reverted to anarchy" ("Graham Greene," *Nation*, CLVII, 1943, p. 19). Against this point of view, however, Derek Traversi says that the Greenelander tends to "tail off, at the moment of definition, into the frustrated and the desultory," and that he is the absurd creation of a sick mind ("Graham Greene: 1. The Earlier Novels," *Twentieth Century*, CXLIX, p. 232). *Even Time* magazine commented, with not too much profundity, that Greene has few "competitors' in the "field" of "Good and Evil" (*Time*, Oct. 29, 1951, p. 104). Jane Howes, on the other hand, is highly suspicious of Greene's version of Good and Evil, claiming that he fails to pursue his **protagonists** through the "gates of hell" that "gulped him down," or into the purgatory where he "got off with only about ten million quarantines" ("Out of the Pit," *Catholic World*, CLXX, 1950, p. 36). Bruce Marshall says that "Graham Greene and Evelyn Waugh make me want to be holy" (*The Commonweal*, LI, 1950, p. 533). In the same magazine, however, Waugh himself expressed grave doubts as to the efficacy of Greene's version of sanctity, at least with regard to *The Heart of the Matter* ("Felix Culpa?" *The Commonweal*, XLVIII, 1948, p. 323). The French critic Jean-H Roy claims that Greene's works are in fact a confirmation of Jean Paul Sartre's views on religion ("Graham Greene ou un christianisme de la damnation," *Les Temps Modernes*, LII, 1950, p. 1519). These few examples show how inconsistent and varied the evaluations of Greene's works are.

REASONS FOR CRITICAL INCONSISTENCIES

The main reason for these inconsistencies is the comparatively recent nature of Greene's acceptance as a major novelist. Although *The Man Within* was published in 1929, for example, and many more works have appeared since, many critics in the United States had never even heard of Graham Greene when *The Power and the Glory* was published in 1940. The reviewer in the Jesuit magazine, America, for example, was not sure whether the author's name was Mr. Graham or Mr. Green (sic), and expressed dismay at the portrayal of a priest who was an alcoholic. It is interesting to note that Greene's reputation had grown so much by the time of the 1946 edition of the novel that Father Harold C. Gardiner wrote an article in America praising the author for his great contribution to Catholic literature ("Taste and Worth," *America*, LXXV, 1946, p. 53). Despite this praise, however, it would be safe to say that Greene's worth as a writer was not fully appreciated, due to a general lack of knowledge of his earlier works. He was known as a good writer of "thrillers," but on the whole critics had ignored the value of such important novels as *It's A Battlefield* (1934) and *England Made Me* (1935). As a result, people tended to view Greene from particular angles without having an over-all view of his real worth as a novelist of major stature.

GENERAL CRITICISM

In an interesting essay called "The Works of Graham Green" (*Horizon*, I, 1940, pp. 367-375), Arthur Calder-Marshall criticizes Greene for his tendency to "reduce everything to a uniform 'vision,'" but does not condemn him for this. He rather praises Greene for recognizing the limitations of his insight, and avoids the trap of dubbing Greene's unique vision a "philosophy." In *Writers of Today* (ed. Denys Val Baker; London: Sedgwick and Jackson, 1946), Walter Allen's essay "Graham Greene" deals with Greene as an Augustinian who concerns himself with the conflict between good and evil, or, in a more specific Catholic terminology, the corruption of human nature by original sin. Mr. Allen deals particularly with the recurring **theme** of the hunted man as it appears in Greene's novels up to and including *The Ministry of Fear*. Both Calder-Marshall and Allen tend to concentrate too intensely on the uniformity of Greene's novels, although they can be forgiven this, due to the limited scope of their essays. Nevertheless this tendency on the part of critics to attack Greene for his "uniformity" is found so generally that it must be taken into consideration in any complete appraisal of his works. W. Gore Allen, for example, in "The World of Graham Greene" (*Irish Ecclesiastical Record*, LXXI, 1949, pp. 42-49) attacks Greene for his lack of individuality in character portrayals. Mr. Allen claims, for example, that Greene's girls are all thin and do not find pleasure in impurity, that his wives are all neurotic, that his policemen are all kind and confused, and that too many of his characters come from the same social milieu, but cannot find their place in society. In a very limited sense, of course, there is an element of truth in Mr. Allen's observations, but they do not take into consideration the diversities underlying many of Greene's uniform types and their characteristics. Coral in Stamboul Train, for example, and Rose in *Brighton Rock* are both thin and find little pleasure in impurity, but there is quite a considerable difference in them as literary figures, although, as we have seen, they are similar types.

GREENE AND HIS FRENCH CRITICS

A little known fact is that Greene has received his most serious criticism in France. The upsurge of French critical interest in Greene came after the Second World War, when *Brighton Rock* was serialized in 1946. It should be pointed out, however, that the immediate French reaction to Greene was one of almost total praise, which was at times overdone. On the other hand, French critics did indeed see his worth as a major literary figure, while English critics have been much slower to appreciate him. Jean-Louis Curtis, for example, in his essay "Impressions de Londres" (*La Table Ronde*, No. 1, 1948, pp. 155-158) is alarmed by the fact that English critics do not seem to appreciate the profundity and moral perceptivity inherent in Greene's works. Some interesting comments on the French reaction to Greene have been made by H. A. Mason in his article "A Note on Contemporary 'Philosophical' Literary Criticism in France" (*Scrutiny*, XVI, 1949, pp. 54-60). Mr. Mason claims that Greene has been accepted readily in France because his novels fit very easily into philosophical patterns already established there, and that French critics "take to" Greene wholeheartedly because they are more interested in meaning than in form. This is a valid observation if literary criticism is to exist devoid of epistemological presuppositions. If criticism were so limited, however, it would indeed be a barren art, and one tends to praise the French for having the acuity of perception, with regard to Greene, that has been so lacking in English and American criticism.

FRENCH BOOKS ON GREENE

Two full-length studies of Greene which have appeared in France are worthy of study. These are Jacques Madaule's *Graham Greene* (Paris: Editions du Temps Present, 1949) and Paul Rostenne's *Graham Greene: témoin des temps tragiques* (Paris: Juilliard, 1949). Madaule's book is the longer of the two, and is particularly useful for the observations it contains on Greene's early novels, but it is a poorly constructed work on the whole, containing many inaccuracies and inconsistencies which detract from its general value. Rostenne's work, on the other hand, is more interesting from the point of view of Greene's position within a particular cultural context. Rostenne omits several of Greene's works, and tends to force some aspects of Greene's writings into his own critical pattern. Nevertheless it is an illuminating and rewarding work, and the chapter entitled "La Vision Greeneienne" is particularly brilliant, illustrating the growing perception Greene has displayed in his works. Rostenne's work is also anomalous, in that it gives us a clear idea of Greene's limitations by concentrating on his literary virtues. The French critic seems to be over-enthusiastic for Greene as a witness of our times, which immediately makes us suspect that Greene does not have as complete a picture as Rostenne would have us believe. As a matter of fact, Rostenne's critical approach to Greene - the approach attacked by H. A. Mason - is one employed by most French critics with regard to Greene's works. This would indeed be detrimental if the French analyzed Greene as a philosopher, and not as a novelist. They have carefully avoided this, however, retaining a traditionally Gallic enthusiasm novel as a for the novel, not as a philosophical treatise.

VARIOUS ASPECTS OF GREENE CRITICISM: PART 1

Greene is the unique type of novelist who can appeal equally well to the "best seller" reading public and to the more selective, intellectual type of audience. This has led to his being discussed on many levels and from many different points of view, and it seems that his works have come to mean anything the individual critic wants them to mean. There are, nevertheless, some common "Greene themes" which have been treated at length by critics, and the student will benefit from an examination of the contradictions existing in the critical appraisals of these themes. There seem to be six major themes, and by examining each in turn, and by studying what critics have said of them, we shall receive a general picture of Greene's works as seen by professional observers.

SIN AND GRACE

General Comments

"Greene's novels invariably present a progression from captivity to freedom, from neurotic compulsion and sin to a point where virtue is at least a critical temptation." In thus summing up a general aspect of Greene's novels, the brilliant Catholic editor and critic William Birmingham opens up several doors to new aspects of a major Greene **theme**: sin and grace. For example, very little public shock has been expressed at sin as it is depicted in Greene's novels, although there have been "orthodox" criticisms such as that of Bruce Marshall: "Greene... portrays the ugliness of a world which no longer even knows what it has fallen from, and sometimes makes even that ugliness seem beautiful because of the author's knowledge of the loveliness of which it is the terrible reverse."

Greene, The Intellectual, and Religion

In 1950 a very illuminating symposium was conducted by the *Partisan Review* on the intellectual and the religious experience. Many contributors held that most literary figures depicted the intellectual's return to religion in an invalid fashion, since these intellectuals are presented without a legitimate, credible religious experience. One criticism levelled against Christian writers was that a marked lack of sincerity makes their writings "unreal" and at times incredible. One Catholic critic, Father Lynch, has discussed quite brilliantly the extent to which sincerity is valid and invalid as a criterion of religious experience, and his views on this are most illuminating for any student who wishes to locate the problem. ("The Partisan Review Symposium," *Thought*, XXV, 1950, pp. 681-691.) On the whole, the *Partisan Review* critics concluded that too often we are presented with details of the battle which rages between man as Christian, and man as man, instead of being given a penetrating insight into what is best described as Christian serenity. In point of fact the whole problem revolves around what is meant by "grace" and consequently "sin," with particular reference, in Greene's case, to Catholic theology. How, then, can we account for the revulsion for Christian, and more specifically for Catholic, literature on the part of many critics? Jean Guitton suggests as an answer that "what is called grace (by modern Christian writers) is not what the old catechism termed habitual or sanctifying grace, which peacefully sublimated our nature," but that grace is rather a destroyer, some supra-human, supra-historical power that shatters the continuity of human existence. It is in this context, then, that we must examine sin and grace as depicted in the novels of Greene. He has been charged, for example, with insincerity and near-heresy, and it is worthwhile examining what various critics have said of this whole problem, particularly with regard to the religious aspects of Greene's novels.

Saint and Sinner in Modern Literature

The criticism of Greene's theological position levelled against him by Bruce Marshall opens up doubts as to the validity of such an "orthodox Catholic" stance when it comes to discussing the modern religious novel. As William Birmingham has pointed out, "It is a cultural problem, not an exclusively religious one. That it exists at all is . . . an indication that something is lacking in contemporary religious culture." The whole problem was posed very neatly by Jean Guitton when he asked once during a lecture whether there still exists something that can be called "human nature." Guitton's own answer is that it does not exist if we consider only contemporary novelists and philosophers, Christian or non-Christian. In Catholic literature, for example, grace is often seen as an improbable bolt out of the blue, but very seldom as something lived through as a state of being. (*Guitton: L'Humanisme et la Grace*, Paris: Editions de Flore, 1950, pp. 130-132.) In this way we find Catholic writers, such as Bloy, Bernanos, Mauriac and Greene depicting characters who are not uplifted by grace, but rather bowled over by it. At this point we should bring in the "sinner-saint" concept, about which much has been written with reference to Greene's novels. Among Catholic writers, Peguy stands out as having concentrated on this idea, and Greene's sinners have often been "sanctified" - by his defenders, more than by Greene himself. It might be well to remember the statement of Father Gerald Vann that "The Sinner Who Looks Like a Saint" plays but a minor role in the history of the Christian drama. In short, it should not be overemphasized, particularly with regard to Greene's novels.

Greene's Personal Theology

It would not be too arrogant to talk of Greene's personal theology," in view of the tremendous controversy that has arisen over some of his ideas. In a penetrating analysis of Greene's works, Derek Traversi claims that Greene's personal religion is "conceived as a purely external act of propitiation" ("Graham Greene: 2., The Later Novels," *Twentieth Century*, CLXIX, 1951, p. 322). Traversi also makes the fascinating observation that a highly personal craving for a spiritual schema creeps into Greene's novels, and that this schema is "willed as an end without being fully accepted or assimilated" ("Graham Greene: 1., The Earlier Novels," *Ibid.,* p. 231). Traversi's analysis tends to be spoiled, however, by his tendency to concentrate too heavily on Greene's personal psychic problems. Another interesting approach is found in an article by Martin Turnell called "The Religious Novel" (*The Commonweal*, LV, 1951, pp. 255-257). In this article, Mr. Turnell gives valuable recognition to the reality of sin in the novels of Greene, claiming that in these works he finds "an incorrigibly romantic attitude towards" sin, created by a "Gidean 'oscillation'" between good and evil. It has been said of Greene (and of Gide) that he maintains and sustains this spiritual tension rather artificially. Yet when we examine *The Power and the Glory*, for example, we find that what William Birmingham calls Greene's "orthodox Manicheism" seems valid and authentic. There might be some argument against Greene in this respect when we examine some aspects of *The Heart of the*

Matter, where, according to Turnell, there is "the use of muddled theology to create an entirely spurious frisson." But any failure to maintain tension validly in this novel is a literary failure, not a theological one. For the theological tension or problem as presented in the story of the police officer is a real one, more powerful because of its validity. This theological tension may not find satisfactory expression in the drama of Scobie's downfall, but this is a fault of the novel, not of the theology it contains. An excellent appraisal of this particular question is found in Marcel More's essay, "The Two Holocausts of Scobie" (translated in *Cross Currents*, No. 2, 1951, pp. 44-63).

Greene And Philosophy

Perhaps the most cogent expression of the problem is found in an essay by Francis X. Connolly, in which he demands that Greene abandon "exaggerated sensibilities" for "the dogmatic truths of philosophy and the hard distinctions of the natural law." Mr. Connolly is hardly suggesting here that budding Catholic authors should take a mandatory course in scholastic philosophy. What he is suggesting, however, is that in approaching the novels of Greene, a critic is perfectly justified in adopting an a-literary approach to its contents, particularly when these contents are uniquely philosophical and theological in nature. In appraising Greene's novels, nevertheless, it should be pointed out that a critic - and particularly a Catholic critic - should resist the temptation to use his own philosophical-cum-theological tenets as a yardstick against which to measure and judge the contents of the works. In other words, if the novelist's story and the critic's ideology are not coextensive, this by no means negates the story's literary merits or validity. In this respect Connolly talks of "the architecture of philosophy," and Turnell makes a plea for the religious decorum as it is found in mediaeval literature. Turnell's position here is interesting, talking as he does of the necessity of the "continuity between . . . religious experience and everyday experience" for the modern novel. Be this as it may, writers like Greene still have tremendous difficulties in facing their quest. It is apparent, for example, that Greene is pursuing "peace," since the word is used time and time again in his novels. The fact that this "peace" is absent from his novels is not a critique of his success or failure, but rather a delimitation of his imaginative powers. It is a fact that a writer can have a deep personal commitment to Catholicism without feeling perfectly at peace with it. This fact should be borne in mind when approaching any critical study of Greene's works, particularly with regard to any "philosophy" they contain.

Greene And The Glorification Of Sin

Jean Guitton's article, to which we have already referred, contains some acute observations and suggestions most useful to anyone wishing to evaluate the religious novel in general and Graham Greene's novels in particular. Guitton, of course, speaks solely as a philosopher and notes that Greene sees grace operating through the worst sins, such as sacrilege and suicide. Guitton sees Greene's method of paving the way to grace as a function achieved "not through the exercise of good, but through the experience of evil." The French philosopher also makes the interesting suggestion that Greene's position stands as a reaction against Catholic bourgeois hypocrisy, which may well lead to a "more subtle pharisaism." He goes on to say that this reaction consists of "a privilege to be, and sort of glory in playing the prodigal." This glorification of the sinner in Greene's novels is something Rostenne talks of as well when he asks: "But what can the clear consciousness of sin mean, if not living permanently in the presence of God?" When discussing the anarchic aspects of Greene's characters, Rostenne also claims that there is a peculiarly alluring quality about this principle of anarchism. He calls it "an instinctive reaction of spiritual anguish," and a necessary weapon against the dangerous "love of order as such." This critical position immediately brings to mind Walter Allen's depiction of Green as an Augustinian rather than a Pelagian. Allen goes on to define an Augustinian as someone who loathes the city of man and craves the city of God, since he sees man as being trapped by original sin and that "natural goodness" is virtually impossible. Allen's critique is oversimplified, however, and is damaging to a clear picture of what Greene-or St. Augustine-is driving at. Here again Allen has committed the critic's sin of pushing Greene's novels into the realm of philosophy, and naturally their contents cannot stand up against the onslaught of pure philosophical dicta. It should be stressed, however, that although Jean Guitton is a professional philosopher, all he does is make philosophic use of Greene's "vision." Wisely he allows that vision to stand as the core of Graham Greene's perceptions as a novelist.

FREEDOM

General Comments

The question of freedom is one central to all of Greene's heroes, and has been a matter of particular concern to French critics. Robert du Parc, for example, in his essay on *The Power and the Glory* ("Saint ou Maudit?" *Etudes*, CCLXX, 1949, pp. 368-381), poses questions which must be faced squarely if we are to appreciate every aspect of Greene as a novelist. Is the whiskey priest a robot, moved by fatality, or is he a free man? Is he a man automatically doomed to hell or is he a saint without knowing it? Are Greene's heroes free or aren't they? General critical response to this important question falls into three main categories, which we will examine briefly.

Paradox and Contradiction

The first of these categories is best expressed by Francis X. Connolly when he claims that Greene's conscious attempt to unite "Catholic themes... with trappings appropriated from determinism... and from abnormal psychology appears to be an ingenious paradox to some, to others a contradiction." According to this school of thought, Greene has in fact created a dilemma, and one which he is unwilling or unable to solve. Connolly claims that by the very fact that they "may both be true is to argue that Greene has not yet answered the full and legitimate demands of his most discriminating readers."

Inevitability of Fatality

The second category finds its best expression in France, especially by the critic Claude-Edmonde Magny ("Graham Greene," *Poesie*, No. 23, 1946, pp. 32-37). According to this point of view, the Greene hero is subject to fatality, "the situation par excellence, since it is based on the fact that man is inseparable from his condition, identified with the place he occupies in the world." Greene's novels say in fact that it is illusory to think that man can elude fatality. In his essay, "Du Rocher de Sysyphe au Rocher de Brighton" (*La Table Ronde*, No. 2, 1948, pp. 306-309), Jean Duche compares the notion held by Camus that mankind is controlled by a tragic destiny with his interpretation of *Brighton Rock*, a view symbolized by the essay's title. Jean-H Roy, on the other hand, holds the same opinion about Greene and Sartre, claiming that Greene's works are a confirmation of Sartre's idea that "if God were a liberator, one could doubt him. He is a jailer." ("L'oeuvre de Graham Greene ou un christianisme de la damnation," *Les Temps Modernes*, LII, 1950, pp. 1513-1519.) According to this second category, religion in the Greene novel is used to trap his heroes and give them the merit of perceiving man's tragic position. Critics who take this point of view fall down, however, when they attempt to equate Greene's vision of grace, sin, and damnation with the terms of non-religious existentialism as expressed in a work like *No Exit*. In Greene, the captivity of the will is a phenomenon existing within the framework of a religious commitment, this commitment being absent from the position held by Sartre or Beckett.

Captivity and Freedom

The third category, and the one which seems most satisfactory, is really an attempt to create a fusion between the first two categories. The French critic, du Parc, claims that the whiskey priest's neurotic despair of self, which renders him "intellectually defenseless . . . in absolute rebellion against the entire spirit of analysis" is transformed by God into a "definitive humility," making him neither a saint, nor accursed, but a very poor man, seized by Christ, and made by his situation an authentic martyr. A similar stance is taken by Marcel More in "The Two Holocausts of Scobie," in which he sees Scobie as being sanctified by the same penetration of compulsion by grace. More regards Scobie as the victim of a neurotic pity leading him into the acceptance of clashing responsibilities for the welfare of his wife and the happiness of his mistress. In this way Scobie is subject to fatality. Yet beyond that, More claims that Scobie's pity is transformed by two holocausts - one on behalf of a dying child and the other for the sake of God in the holocaust of his own damnation - into sanctifying love. It is interesting to note that Greene himself disagrees with much of More's analysis ("Propos de table avec Graham Greene," *Dieu Vivant*, No. 16, 1950, pp. 129 & 134). Greene observes that the French translation of *The Heart of the Matter* is inaccurate, in that it makes God the object of Scobie's last words, "Dear God, I love," whereas Greene means the words to be deliberately ambiguous ("Lettre de Graham Greene," *Dieu Vivant*, No. 17, 1950, p. 152).

Louis Beirnaert, on the other hand, considers the dialectic of freedom and subjection to psychic deformity in the Greene hero ("Does Sanctification Depend on Psychic Structure?" *Cross Currents*, No. 2, 1951, pp. 39-43). Beirnaert says that Greene's characters are examples of the people "who fall and will fall again; those who will weep to the end, not because they have knocked too loudly at a door, but because they have committed . . . sin-sordid, unmentionable." This essay by Beirnaert and one by Jean Rimaud ("Psychologists versus Morality," *Cross Currents*, No. 2, 1951, pp. 26-38) are particularly useful since they tackle the moral and theological implications of man's conditioned freedom. Critics must at least be aware of this problem if they wish to make any kind of over-all appraisal of Greene's novels.

There is yet another sub-division of this third category, one which has been expressed by Paul Rostenne. He says that Greene's works represent "rather than a psychology of fatality... a psychology of the risk of damnation . . . a psychology of the situation of the sinner." The question is not whether fatality exists in the lives of the Greene heroes - their very helplessness seems to suggest that at least-but whether the liberty which they see available to them is illusory or not. Rostenne claims that it is not, and he does this by making the distinction between the ways someone can be controlled by his situation and the ways that the critical power of grace can transform the sinner subject to fatality. Two good examples of this are found in Rose

(*Brighton Rock*) and in the whiskey priest (*The Power and the Glory*). In both these characters, their fidelity to vocation results from a conscious willingness to be acted upon. These characters see that "something must be done" (Rostenne) and that only their acceptance will achieve what is to be done. Again, Raven in *This Gun for Hire* and Pinkie in *Brighton Rock* are sinners whom fatality has imprisoned in a closed morality. This fatality is open to the grace of God by the very fact that sin implies a consciousness of God.

NATURAL AND SUPERNATURAL ORDERS

The **theme** of flight and pursuit is one which runs through Greene's major novels and, in tracing this **theme**, Walter Allen says that in *Brighton Rock*, "pursuer and pursued now exist in a separate universe of belief." Referring to the same novel, Neville Braybrooke sees a unique form of Catholic discrimination among the characters ("Graham Greene," *Envoy*, III, 1950, pp. 10-23). Connolly goes further than this by saying that Greene creates an opposition between the natural and supernatural orders which conflicts with reality. He says that "when the philosophical implications are pressed too hard, the contrast distorts reality. Right and wrong are not really opposed to good and bad . . . " The fictional device employed by Greene is quite a legitimate one, for Greene sees a gulf between the secular and nonsecular orders, and heightens this gulf for the sake of conflict within the novel.

The nature of this conflict is worthy of examination, and the most interesting character to study in this respect is Ida Arnold in *Brighton Rock*, whom William Birmingham calls "the flat caricature of the secular world." If we look at her as Greene depicts her, she represents to us not a composite of all people who owe allegiance to no church, but rather as an example of a particular "secular world." Ida's character is dominated by inadequacy of moral sensibility, and she is not to be viewed as an exponent of some vague kind of "natural goodness." She also has a unique role to play in the general structure of the novel, apart from being the pursuer in the flight and pursuit motif. As Mr. Birmingham has pointed out so well in his appraisal of this particular question, "It [*Brighton Rock*] is a dramatic novel in which time in the sense of the cyclic rhythm of the world is used to point up the dynamism of time in the sense of a preparation for eternity." Ida reacts "in tune" with the world, its pace and its rhythms, and functions in response to external stimuli, while herself devoid of values. She has "only got to wait" to achieve her aim and, having dedicated herself to time, she is unaffected by it. Time, on the other hand, rushes Pinkie and Rose to the edge of eternity, because these two characters have chosen good and evil. Mr. Birmingham's observations on this issue would be hard to refute: "because eternity is significant, time is powerful. The drama of the novel depends on the latter notion of time and... Ida is necessary in order to give it proper emphasis." On the whole, it can be said that the distinction of the two orders is real and is probably necessary for Greene, who is operating simultaneously on both the religious and artistic levels. This motif is reiterated in Greene's major novels from *It's A Battlefield* on.

VARIOUS ASPECTS OF GREENE CRITICISM: PART 2

INTERPERSONAL COMMUNICATION

General Comments

This is one of the most interesting, and in some ways complex, aspects of Greene's novels, and is therefore worthy of some detailed comment. The Greene hero is, as we have seen, bound by sin and neurosis. It would follow, therefore, that there must be a marked lack of interpersonal communication in his novels. Yet the fundamental breakdown takes the form of the inability on the part of his major characters to communicate with themselves, and this has not been widely discussed. What have been given wider treatment, however, are the sexual attitudes which exist in his novels. These attitudes are themselves symbolic of non-communication, together with the social isolation of Greene's protagonists. And all this is linked to the hostility toward the secular order and to the operation of grace as it appears in the major novels.

The Priest, Scobie, and Communication

Speaking of the priest in *The Power and the Glory*, Robert du Parc says: "Intellectually defenseless, he reveals himself in absolute rebellion against the entire spirit of analysis, unable to discern the true motives which animate him." This is in fact the essential core of the problem besetting the priest. He is riddled with guilt feelings, but is unable to determine their cause. He associates his love for his illegitimate child, for example, with his fornication, thereby linking the inevitability of his love with the inevitability of his damnation. Du Parc points out that the priest is prepared for martyrdom by his "definitive humility," which is a despair of his self, not of God. Rostenne also remarks that this preparation is the result of his "fidelity to the essential," namely, his priesthood. But the priest does not possess the self-awareness necessary to evaluate his experiences and act upon that evaluation.

A similar problem is at the center of Scobie's dilemma. He reveals himself throughout the novel as being as much out of communication with himself as the whiskey priest is. More remarks that the lies Scobie tells his wife through pity have "all the symptoms of a true psychic disease," yet Greene gives us no shred of evidence that Scobie is aware of this. More also makes the illuminating observation that the opposite is in fact true, that Scobie's lies do not trouble him at all until the full, dreadful implication of their consequences begin to become evident to him.

Communication And The Man Within

Jacques Madaule is the only critic who gave Greene's first novel, *The Man Within*, careful consideration and a detailed analysis.

Unfortunately, he missed the fact that this idea of the breakdown of communication with the self is central to the novel's meaning and that the allegorical plot contains the seed of many of Greene's later and more mature ideas. The novel's hero, Francis Andrews, has the problem of determining who he is. Confused by his hatred for his cruel father and by the romantic dreams engendered by Carlyon, he is at the same time unnerved by the voice of the "inner critic," which will accept neither attitude. The love for Elizabeth, which wins out, may well represent the hero's discovery that this "inner critic" is in fact his real self and that the complete exercise of personal liberty comes through a commitment to faith. The idea of self-communication is explicitly stated in *The Man Within*, although not so satisfactorily as in his later works. It should be remembered that this idea is common to all Greene's works.

Two Problems Concerning Communication

Two problems arise here through this question of communication:

1. The first problem is solved when we accept the fact that Greene's characters are unable to communicate with themselves. Greene employs the useful method of the dramatic soliloquy to advance the actions of each novel, and to portray to us the condition of a soul which does not know its own identification. One must be careful, however, not to accept quite literally what a character says, or even the words he uses. Evelyn Waugh, for example, pounced on Scobie's use of the word "love," and, equating it with "pity," as expressed by Scobie, pointed an accusing finger at Greene on the grounds of blasphemy.

2. The second problem is closely connected to the nature of Waugh's protest. Referring to *The Power and the Glory*, du Parc observes that while the whiskey priest's dilemma may be convincing, "perhaps the doctrine of Graham Greene is subject to caution," Greene in other words seems too willing to surrender to action devoid of accurate introspection, which ends up in the author's being unsure of the state of the priest's soul. In this respect, Greene himself replies to a question by More that he regards Scobie's first fault his transgression as a police officer-burning the contraband letter ("Propos de table avec Graham Greene," *Dieu Vivent*, No. 16, 1950, pp. 127-137). More had claimed that the lies Scobie tells through pity are the manifestations of the psychic ailment which eventually destroys him. Greene's view of the novel is that Scobie represents "the Just," despite these lies, and that his collapse begins when he extends his pity and the accompanying dishonesty beyond the family circle. At this point, of course, it is obvious to suggest that a creative writer is not necessarily his own best critic. It is highly probable, also, that the psychological insight Greene shows in his character portrayals is not completely conscious. This may well account for the inconsistencies between action and statement in *The Heart of the Matter*, which William Birmingham describes as "an eschatological puzzler, but not ultimately an integrated work of art."

Sexual Response and Communication

Sexual response is an important part of interpersonal communication for Greene's characters. As such it has been often neglected for the striking traumas that have made this response hateful to many of these characters. Derek Traversi has recorded most of these traumatic events, together with occasions on which Greene himself shows signs of displaying personal sexual revulsion. As a critic, Traversi feels that Greene has not made "of religion something more than a projection of accidental and personal qualities," and therefore confines his own judgments on Greene's novels to them. He regards "the lack of correspondence between the inner and outer man" the chief tragedy and fault of *England Made Me*, for example, since the characters "tail off at the moment of definition, into the frustrated and the desultory."

While this criticism holds for *England Made Me*, the criteria Traversi employs seem inadequate when he deals with more mature works like *Brighton Rock*, which he defines "as the projection of an obscure relationship between personal inhibitions and an objective structure of belief." With Traversi's observations we must take into consideration his tendency to equate Greene with his characters and to neglect the importance of a psychic problem on a moral level. If we do that, we will find in his comments some useful delineations of sexual attitudes as they exist in Greene's novels. We would not go so far as Harry Sylvester, however, who says that Pinkie, in *Brighton Rock*, displays "a kind of chastity, warped and misinformed, whose effect can be worse than lust," and that Greene is commenting here "on the possible effects of Puritanism on our adolescents' attitude toward sex" ("Graham Greene," *The Commonweal*, XXXIII, 1940, p. 12). Greene in fact uses sexual activity in his novels primarily as a means of communication, despite the Manicheism or Jansenism of his anatomical metaphors, and despite the sexual attitudes of many of Greene's characters. It is hard to agree with Madaule, too, who revolves his interpretation of sexual activity in Greene's novels around what he calls "a strange cult of virginity." William Birmingham's answer to

Madaule's theory seems much more plausible: "Here is rather a willed spiritual conception of sexual behavior as communication between persons, played out against a background of negative and often revolting metaphor."

Rostenne's view of what is wrong with Pinkie seems extremely valid: he is so proud that he must detest all human contact, and he uses his virginity as a weapon of this pride, since his pride would be humbled and his proud isolation shattered, were he to accept a sexual relationship, even on the level of sin. Sexual sins in Greene's novels serve to pinpoint a breakdown in interpersonal communication, since sexual relations take place as acts of attempted communication. Even in the Catholic context of sin, the sexual act is a gesture made toward communication, and can threaten to destroy the isolation a character has chosen for himself. This is exactly what happens to Pinkie. What can be said, then, about the charges of puritanism that have been levelled so often against Greene, particularly by Catholic critics? The puritanism in Greene lies in his choice of **metaphor** in his expression of all bodily activities, not only sexual relationships. When this is appropriate to the particular character, it is successful. This can be said of *It's A Battlefield*, although it is less successful in *England Made Me*, *Brighton Rock*, and *The Power and the Glory*. When we consider Scobie's relations with his wife and mistress in this light, we can see the reason for the weakness in Greene's writing: man and **metaphor** are not compatible.

Social Aspects of Communication

We spoke earlier about the conflict between the secular and religious orders in Greene's novels, and this is similar to the collapse of communication on a social level as it appears in his works. There is one important distinction, however, which must be elucidated. While the secular man is dangerous, he is dangerous unconsciously. The man dedicated to the social order-Greene's recurring policeman, for example-is not so much dangerous as frustrated. While he is doing his best in terms of the only existence he thinks available to him, he feels helpless in the face of society's chaos and corruption. Note, however, how the opposite type of character in a Greene novel is equally as impotent. The outcast with no commitment to society other than to rebel against it may, like Raven in *This Gun for Hire*, accomplish what he wants-but it is at the cost of his life. In this way, the criminal and the policeman are very similar in Greene's novels. Neither type is "secularized" in the same way as Ida Arnold is, for in both types there exists the seed of a genuine spirituality.

The Outcast and Communication

Considerable critical attention has been given to the outcast in his criminal guise, as depicted in the Greene novel. Rostenne says that "There is no doubt that the anarchism of Raven and of Pinkie is a form of corruption. But it is also necessary to add with Greene: corruptio optimi est pessima." According to Max-Pol Fouchet, the outcast is a dramatic figure, for he does not commune with anyone else; and the dialogue here is "between the characters and a Supreme Witness," the violence being consequently Elizabethan in its force ("Graham Greene," *Revue de Paris*, No. 307, 1950, p. 61). Jean-H Roy claims that this isolated Greene-lander interests the existentialist especially because of his "absolute and gratuitous violence." Madaule contends that he rebels against a society which "exists to protect a minority of haves against the assaults . . . of an immense army of have - nots." In Walter Allen's view, he is combatting "the world of economic man at his most urbanized and atomized." He is the central figure in Greene's "thrillers," a novel form which, according to Rostenne, "strives to awaken in the reader the strongest and most basic emotions, by rediscovering primitive man in the heart of civilization."

Anarchism and Greene Criticism

It is understandable that critics should be preoccupied with Greene's depiction of the terrible isolation found in extracommunal existence. Yet this preoccupation with what Zabel calls "the atom of the lonely man" in "a world of mindless and psychotic brutality," does not do the novelist justice. Quite objectively, the "anarchist" in this sense is the **protagonist** of only one Greene novel, *Brighton Rock*, and does not appear as the hero in any other important novel. If the critic concentrates on anarchism in *It's A Battlefield*, he will miss the point that Greene is presenting a society more complex and more capable of objective emotions. As an aside, it should be pointed out that this notion of society underlies some of the religious attitudes inherent in the Greene novel.

Society and It's a Battlefield

According to V. S. Pritchett, the **theme** of *It's A Battlefield* is "the pursuit of the Shadow, Justice" ("It's A Battlefield," *Spectator*, CLII, 1934, p. 206). The fact that this work depicts people operating within the natural order has been overlooked by subsequent critics. Although Neville Braybrooke calls it "A battle between material and spiritual values," he misses the point that *It's A Battlefield* plays a significant part in determining the direction Greene's novels were to take. The two main characters, an Assistant Commissioner of the C.I.D. and a chief clerk, each a searcher for the certitude of justice, take alternate roads, one by way of commitment to the social order (the Assistant Commissioner) and the other by way of revolt against it (the chief clerk). The point is that the choice worth studying here is not so much the clerk's-that of anarchism-as it is the Commissioner's-that of conformity. The Commissioner, who is left identified with his job, has no certainty that it is worth doing. The attitude toward society underlying Greene's religious thinking is also seen in the position of the one religious figure in the book, an Anglican priest who withdraws from participation in society. This novel says, in fact, that society is indeed a battlefield whose outlines are invisible, and which is meaningless to us. We have three choices: we can rebel against it, we can commit ourselves to it, or we can withdraw from it. The only thing of which we can be certain is that society itself will have no issue. This is an important concept of society which we find in all of Greene's novels, namely that it is there, but that it has no validity. In this respect, it is worth remembering a comment made about Greene by Mauriac, to the effect that the English novelist seems more attracted by the hidden Church than by the Church of Pomp ("La Puissance et la Gloire," *Renascence*, I, 1949, p. 26).

PITY

General Comments

Much of the modern novel is infected by the morality of pity, and the concept is very important in any consideration of Graham Greene's novels. In William Birmingham's words, "It is a reflex ethic of opposition to pain and it leads modern man into good and evil." In itself it is a legitimate concept, but it cannot exist by itself. Pity demands the discipline of an ascetic morality and then it can be transformed, by grace, into charity. But as we have seen, pity and charity are closely allied, sometimes with terrifying results. Scobie's collapse in *The Heart of the Matter* is an excellent example of this. There is indeed a world of difference between the man who pities and the man who loves, and it is essential that we recognized the difference.

Pity in Greene's Novels

W. H. Auden draws attention to the fact that "in book after book, Graham Greene analyzes the vice of pity, that corrupt **parody** of love and compassion which is so insidious and deadly for sensitive natures" ("The Heresy of Our Time," *Renascence*, I, 1949, pp. 23-24). He goes on to say that pity is essentially egotistic, since "behind pity for another lies self-pity, and behind self-pity lies cruelty." In these succinct statements, Auden analyzes the question of pity in Greene's novels, and they are worth remembering, in view of the surfeit of banal criticism which has appeared on this subject. Mary McCarthy, for example, says that pity in Greene's novels is not a major emotion, and that any of his characters dominated by pity is consequently unreal. She also accuses Greene of being "pious and insincere" in his use of pity. This point of view seems to be reinforced strongly by many eminent Catholic theologians who regard pity as a "pious" emotion, in a pejorative sense, But let us stress the fact that Greene is not a theologian, but a novelist, and as such his texts must be examined primarily from a literary standpoint. The overstressing of the "theology" of Greene's pity led Evelyn Waugh into his confused statements on *The Heart of the Matter* and Sister Mariella Gable into her myopic critiques of pity as portrayed in *Brighton Rock* and *The Heart of the Matter* (*This is Catholic Fiction*, New York: Sheed and Ward, 1948).

Two Divergent Views on Pity

The two major and opposite attitudes to Greene's use of pity
are synthesized for us in the dialogue between Marcel More and
Raymond Jouve on the relation of love and pity as they exist
in the character of Scobie ("La damnation de Scobie?" *Etudes*,
CCLXIII, 1949, pp. 164-177). More concentrates on Scobie's
neurasthenia and Jouve on his freedom and culpability, two
critical attitudes which have a meeting point from which we can
examine the pity-love relationship.

1. Both critics agree that Scobie's human relationships
    are all fashioned by pity, and that this pity prompts
    actions which are in fact means of escaping reality. Their
    respective positions are then outlines. More holds that
    Scobie "is too weak, psychically speaking, to endure the
    sight of another's suffering" and that the resultant guilt
    feelings drive him to assume responsibility for the lives
    of others. Jouve says that Scobie is trying to "dispense
    with God, to wrestle with God," and to replace God by
    himself.

2. Both critics agree on Scobie's self-damnation as the
    consummation of the novel, and make particular note
    of the "holocaust of damnation" motivated by love.
    Jouve, however, does not try to pass any judgment on
    the efficacy of Scobie's sacrifice, while More takes the
    definite stance that it is an act of love, and as such, it
    is enough to save Scobie's soul. More's position would
    imply, therefore, that pity automatically is transformed
    to love when the self is forgotten in the act of sacrifice.
    William Birmingham has pointed out quite rightly that
    "Jouve, since he is not concerned with proving Scobie's

salvation, might have taken into consideration what More has ignored."

This naturally raises the essential question of whether the extraordinary act of love demanded by the holocaust of damnation is psychologically in keeping with Scobie's character or, in fact, with the condition of his soul. The action of the novel suggests that the noble intention of such a self-sacrifice-namely the desire to surrender everything for God-does not seem to be a logical part of Scobie's spiritual or psychological make-up. Greene undoubtedly intended Scobie's suicide to be such an act of love, but from the reader's point of view, all we see is Scobie extending his pity to God. We must make up our own minds as to whether this pity has undergone a metamorphosis and ended up as love.

Greene, Camus, and Pity

An attempt to show the affinity between Graham Greene and Albert Camus has been made by Henry A. Grubbs in his essay "Albert Camus and Graham Greene" (*Modern Language Quarterly*, X, 1949, pp. 33-42). Grubbs' essay is illuminating for the way he juxtaposes the element of pity in the novels of both writers. His vision is somewhat restricted, however, by his accentuation of the influence of Camus by Greene. There is, in fact, a tendency to attribute the advent of the post-war French "absurd" school of literature to Greene's position as a prophet of modern man's helplessness-an interpretation of Greene which is, of course, erroneous. Grubbs points out correctly that in *The Power and the Glory* it is the lieutenant, not the priest, who is motivated by pity. What Grubbs does not recognize, however, is that the pity which motivates the lieutenant is the same pity which motivates Tarrou, "the saint without God" in Camus' *The Plague.*

Meursault in *The Stranger* operates in a state of protest against universals. In *The Plague*, however, Camus creates a morality of pity for a man who has nothing else-pity seen as a hopeless and eternal fight against pain. The same kind of pity dominates Ida in *Brighton Rock*. To her, right and wrong are equated with pleasure and pain. Pity informs the lieutenant in *The Power and the Glory* and prompts his total commitment to the State, since, in his view, "suffering is wrong." The lieutenant is even willing to inflict pain in order to alleviate the pain of social ills.

This recalls the views on pity expressed by Auden, who also notes that Arthur Rowe and the Nazis he fights have one thing in common-murder. Rowe commits murder to alleviate pain, and those he fights show cruelty to someone who blocks their way to achieving an ideal abstraction. In the novels of Camus and Greene, pity is the morality of those without God, but of the two, Greene reveals pity in its tragic dimensions. It should be noted that in Greene's works, the self-pity behind pity for others is a symptom of the modern tendency to lament man's lot while indulging in the luxury of a self-pity concealed behind a front of respectability.

TECHNIQUE

General Comments

From the point of view of technique, Walter Allen has noted Greene's indebtedness to the cinema. "To [his] presentation of the contemporary scene he brought a swift, nervous . . . style and a technique of montage which owes much to the film." Evelyn Waugh also has observed that "the affinity to the camera's eye is everywhere apparent." Greene records events like a concealed movie camera, often ensuring that the actors are unaware of what is happening. Connolly discusses Greene's camera technique, which transforms the matter of daily life into the matter of a novel. It is important for us to recognize the fact that the camera, which was once a mechanical recorder of events, has assumed definite moral attributes. The modern camera not only selects detail, but also gives an opinion on the moral significance of what it selects. We should remember this fact in studying the techniques used by Greene in his novels.

Greene and the Narrator

There is great difficulty, however, in meeting the problem of moral statement in the novel, and Greene overcomes this by having a concealed, objective narrator reveal the inner man. Neville Braybrooke has gone so far as to say that this is quite a major contribution to the art of novel writing. "His technique is simple: it is the adaptation of the dramatic soliloquy to the confines of the novel: in the process histrionics are abandoned, so that one has the impression not of somebody declaiming his thoughts to the world at large, but of somebody whispering his inmost doubts and conflicts to one by telephone." It is an interesting and useful method, since the author can achieve objectivity while retaining freedom in the portrayal of conscience. Braybrooke illustrates the point he is making by comparing parallel selections from Another Mexico and *The Power and the Glory*, showing how Greene very deftly turns fact into fiction.

Structure of Greene's Novels

Greene displays a highly developed dramatic sense in the structure of his novels. Time is always essential, and the plot's progress depends a great deal on the interplay of fate and freedom in the actions of his characters. A sense of the acceleration of time creates a concomitant sense of urgency in the action. Greene's "camera-eye" point of view allows him to shift from one scene to another, suspending action in one place, while taking it up in another. Note that the novels before *The Power and the Glory* take up only a short space of time, characters being introduced immediately before or after the main action that is going to alter their lives. From that moment on, there is almost a nervous motion leading to the eventual solution. In *The Power and the Glory*, however, Greene is obliged to use a longer time span because of the nature of the plot. Arthur Calder-Marshall points out that since the pace of the novel is that of a "thriller," the total effect is "dissipated in the confusion of detail," and the amount of action makes "the priest's open-eyed return to martyrdom . . . capricious." The opinion is the result of the critic's having defined the novel's **theme** as "epic," and should therefore be taken with some reservations. The judgment is nevertheless important in raising the question of how swiftly a dramatic novel can move. In fact, Greene's use of pace in the novel could scarcely be excelled. From the first paragraph he establishes a state of tension which he sustains throughout the novel with remarkable consistency.

Greene's Style

An adequate and satisfying study of Greene's style is yet to be made. The staccato element in his writing has been compared to Hemingway, while his descriptive passages are somehow reminiscent of Conrad. But one can overdo comparisons, and it is safe to say that Greene has developed a style that is uniquely his own. Waugh says that it is "not a specifically literary style at all. The words are functional . . . simply mathematical signs for his thought." A study of Greene's style in his essays as compared with his novels seems to refute Waugh's judgment, although it is admittedly rather difficult to pinpoint precisely why his style is in fact literary.

Critics often seem to revel in attacking Greene for his use of metaphors and similes. Mary McCarthy, for example, attacks him for his use of "words with churchly connotations" which, she claims, create a religious atmosphere which is not justified in the light of the novel's action. Vernon Young says that a "mixture of sensate aversions and autohypnotic pity . . . deforms his novels," and that "the tragic (or rather, pathetic) flaw in Greene's literary character is projected through his most conspicuously mechanical stylistic device, the negative simile," which are "verbalized reflexes of the will to misery." On the whole, it is important to note that Greene's style is subservient to the meaning and action of his novels. Greene attempted to use extravagant language in his first three novels, which Neville Braybrooke calls "European Westerns." As Greene's technique matured, however, his style became more rigorous, and the main problem in his new novels was establishing and sustaining a tone relevant to his themes. R. W. Flint claims that when Greene is writing well "he can do this in the act of advancing his action, but he more frequently resorts to a relentless hammering of artistic effects." ("Recent Fiction," *Hudson Review*, I, 1949-50, p. 592). Flint is somewhat overstating the case, for Greene's novels do depend on something more than a clever blending of words, metaphors, and similes. These latter devices are certainly congruous with Greene's **themes** and approach. What does constitute a disconcerting and detracting aspect of his devices, is the definite Manichean flavor of his metaphors. William Birmingham's words on this matter are worth recording and remembering: "This sublevel of opposition between matter and spirit as good and evil often overrides the philosophically and theologically just 'war between two eternities' which delimits his vision."

Conclusion

Having covered six aspects of Greene's novels, with particular reference to various critical views which have been expressed, it should be stated that a great deal of work is yet to be done on his fiction. For example, a complete and embracing appraisal is yet to be made of Greene's place, in what for lack of a better expression we will call "Catholic fiction." And, as we saw earlier, it is necessary to recognize the fact that there is indeed such a thing as a "Catholic writer," one whose own religious commitment has relevance to every aspect of his work. The criticism of Greene in this respect has been inadequate so far, due to the tendency of critics to approach his novels from a purely theological or philosophical point of view. Greene criticism has to take an over-all view of his works to save them from what Birmingham calls "the rebirth-of-Catholic-letters bandwagon," and to make his religious works acceptable and credible to those who are suspicious of Catholicism when linked with fiction. Then, and only then, will Greene's true stature as one of the finest contemporary novelists be measured.

BIBLIOGRAPHY

· ·

Allen, Walter, "Graham Greene," *Writers of Today*, Denys Val Baker, ed., 1946.

Allen, W. Gore, "The World of Graham Greene," *Irish Ecclesiastical Record*, LXXI (1949), 42-49.

Allott, K., and M. Farris, *The Art of Graham Greene* (1951).

Auden, W. H., "The Heresy of Our Time," *Renascence*, I (1949), 23-24.

Battcock, Marjorie, "The Novels of Graham Greene," *The Norseman*, XIII (1955), 45-52.

Beirnaert, Louis, "Does Sanctification Depend on Psychic Structure?" *Cross Currents*, No. 2 (1951), 39-43.

Birmingham, William, "Graham Greene Criticism: A Bibliographical Study," *Thought*, XXVI (1952), 72-100.

Braybrooke, Neville, "Graham Greene," *Envoy*, III (1950), 10-23.

_____, "Graham Greene as Critic," *The Commonwealth*, LIV (1951), 312-314.

Calder-Marshall, Arthur, "The Works of Graham Greene," *Horizon*, I (1940), 367-375.

Choisy, Maryse, "Psychoanalysis and Catholicism," *Cross Currents*, No. 3 (1951), 75-90.

Codey, Regina, "Notes on Graham Greene's Dramatic Technique." *Approach*, No. 17 (1955), 23-27.

Connolly, Francis, X., "Inside Modern Man: The Spiritual Adventures of Graham Greene," *Renascence*, I (1949), 16-24.

Curtis, Jean-Louis, "Impressions de Londres," *La Table Ronde*, No. 1 (1948), 155-158.

De Vitis, A., *Graham Greene*, 1964.

Duche, Jean, "Du Rocher de Sysyphe au Rocher de Brighton," *La Table Ronde*, No. 2 (1948), 306-309.

Flint, R. W., "Recent Fiction," *Hudson Review*, I (1948-49), 590-596.

Fouchet, Max-Pol, "Graham Greene," *Revue de Paris*, CCCVII (1950), 59-68.

Gable, Sister Mariella, *This is Catholic Fiction* (1949).

Gardiner, Harold C., "Taste and Worth," *America*, LXXV (1946), 53.

Grubbs, Henry A., "Albert Camus and Graham Greene," *Modern Language Quarterly*, X (1949), 33-42.

Guitton, Jean, "Y a-t-il encore une nature humaine?" *L'Humanisme et la Grace* (Paris, 1950), 125-142.

Hoehn, M., ed., *Catholic Authors*, I.

Howes, Jane, "Out of the Pit," *Catholic World*, CLXX (1950), 36-40.

Jouve, Raymond, "La Damnation de Scobie?" *Etudes*, CCLXIII (1949), 164-177.

Kunkel, Francis Leo, *The Labyrinthine Ways of Graham Greene, 1960.*

Madaule, Jacques, *Graham Greene* (Paris, 1946).

Magny, Claude-Edmonde, "Graham Greene," *Poesie*, No. B2 (1946), 32-37.

Marshall, Bruce, "Graham Greene and Evelyn Waugh," *The Commonwealth*, LI (1950), 551-553.

Mason, H. A., "A Note on Contemporary 'Philosophical' Literary Criticism in France," *Scrutiny*, XVI (1949), 54-60.

Mauriac, Francois, "La Puissance et la Gloire," *Renascence*, I (1949), 25-27.

_____, *Men I Hold Dear.*

McCarthy, Mary, "Graham Greene and the Intelligentsia," *Partisan Review*, XI (1944), 228-230.

Mesnet, Marie Beatrice, *Graham Greene and the Heart of the Matter (1954).*

More, Marcel, "The Two Holocausts of Scobie," in *Cross Currents of Psychiatry and Catholic Morality*, William Birmingham and Joseph E. Cunneen, eds., reprinted from *Cross Currents*, No. 2 (1951).

O'Brien, Conor Cruise, "Graham Greene: The Anatomy of Pity" and Mr. Greene's Battlefield," in *Maria Cross*, (1954).

O'Faolain, Sean, "Graham Greene: I Suffer: Therefore I Am," in *The Vanquishing Hero: Studies in Novelists of the Twenties* (London, 1956).

Parc, Robert du, "Saint ou Maudit?" *Etudes*, CCLX (1949), 368-381.

Pritchett, V. S., "It's A Battlefield," *Spectator*, CLII (1934), 206.

Rimaud, Jean, "Psychologists versus Morality," *Cross Currents*, No. 2 (1951), 26-38.

Rostenne, Paul, *Graham Greene: témoin des temps tragiques (Paris, 1949).*

Roy, Jean-H., "L'oeuvre de Graham Greene ou un christianisme de la damnation," *Les Temps Modernes*, LII (1950), 1513-1519.

Sackville-West, Edward, "The Electric Hare," *The Monk*, VI (1951), 141-147.

"Shocker," *Time*, October 29, 1951, 98-104.

Stratford, Philip, *Faith and Fiction* (1964).

Sylvester, Harry, "Graham Greene," *The Commonweal*, XXIII (1940), 11-30.

Traversi, Derek, "Graham Greene: 1. The Earlier Novels" and "Graham Greene: 2. The Later Novels," *Twentieth Century*, CXLIX (1951), 318-328.

Turnell, Martin, "The Religious Novel," *The Commonweal*, LV (1951), 55-57.

Waugh, Evelyn, "Felix Culpa," *The Commonweal*, XLVIII (1948), 322-325.

Wyndham, Francis, *Graham Greene* (1955).

Young, Vernon, "Hell on Earth: Six Versions," *Hudson Review* (1949-50), 311-317.

Zabel, Morton D., "Graham Greene," *Nation*, CLVII (1943), 18-20.

_____, in *Forms of Modern Fiction*, W. V. O'Connor, ed., 1959.